Applied Iridology and Herbology

Donald R. Bamer B.S., D.C.

DEDICATION

This book is dedicated to my wife Ann and daughter Brenda, for their help and understanding of the long hours required in the preparation of a book of this nature.

Also, a special dedication to my assistant Charla, whom without her dedication, long hours, and patience this book would have never been completed.

Neither the author nor the publisher, directly or indirectly, dispense medical advice. If you use the information contained herein without the advice of your physician, you are prescribing for yourself, (which is your constitutional right), and the author and publisher assume no responsibility.

© 1982 Donald R. Bamer
ISBN 0-89557-053-X

All rights reserved. No part of this book may be reproduced by any method without the written permission of the author and the publisher.

Published in the United States of America
by Woodland Health Books
P.O. Box 1422 • Orem, Utah 84603

Dr. Donald Bamer, B. S. D. C., has a successful holistic practice in Tulsa, Oklahoma. He is a highly acclaimed Chiropractic Physician, Nutritionalist, Herbalist, and Clinical Iridologist. He has done an extensive indepth study of the latest research findings from Germany in the field of Iridology.

He is well known among the professionals and the public for his work as a national lecturer and author of several professional papers on diagnostic Iridology.

Dr. Bamer attended the European Division of the University of Maryland and Universities in California. He holds National and State Certificates in both the Basic and Clinical Sciences.

He graduated from Palmer College of Chiropractic with honors. While at Palmer College he supervised diagnostic and Clinical procedures. He also worked with a team of clinical psychologists in a research program with autistic children through the University of California at Santa Barbara.

Dr. Bamer is the president of the National Iridology Association. He is also a member of the American Chiropractic Association, American Chiropractic Clinical Nutrition Association, American Chiropractic Council on Neurology, National Association of Naturopathic Physicians and an active member of the International Academy of Preventative Medicine.

Contents

Chapter I Introduction to Iridology and Applied Herbology 11

Chapter II How this Phenomenom Works and Interpreting the Signs 21

Chapter III Significant Iridology Findings 31
    A. Pupillary Changes
       • A quick evaluation for hypoglycemia
    B. Hypo-Acidic Stomach
       • Most people are unaware of it
    C. Hyper-Acidic Stomach
       • Potential ulcers
       • There is something better than anti acids!
    D. Toxic Colon
       • Death Begins Here
       • Cleansing Formulas
    E. Radii Solaris
       • Radials from the sun
       • A sign known by many
    F. Radial Furrows
       • Toxic Sediments
       • What they indicate and how to remove them
    G. Parasites
       • Indicative Sign and Probabilities
       • Natural Remedies
    H. Diverticuli
       • What they are and how to get rid of them
    I. Hyper-Acidic Tissues
       • Possible early staage of arthritis
       • How to balance body acids
    J. Hyper-Alkaline Tissues
       • Potential Heart Attacks
       • Mineral deficiencies
    K. Psychological Stress Lines
       • Potential Nervous Breakdowns
       • Vit. and Mineral Deficiencies

L. Pathological Polychromia
- Organ Damage at a Glance
- Turn the Green Eyes Blue - Again

M. Sectorial Hetechromia
- What goes in doesn't *always* come out!

N. Lymphatic Tophi
- Bodies Ability to Fight Infection
- How to increase resistance to disease

O. Arcus Senilis
- Senility Potential and how to prevent it

P. Hypercholesterosis
- The beginning of hardening of the arteries
- How to prevent or correct it

Q. Toxic Circulatory System
- When the circulatory system turns into a *sewer* system
- How to clean up the blood

R. Skin
- Pimples start on the inside not the outside
- Natural remedies for beautiful skin

S. Healing Crises
- Just when you think you are cured
- What to expect and how to manage it

Chapter IV Major Organs and Natural Remedies   71
    A. Heart
    B. Lungs
    C. Liver
    D. Kidneys
    E. Nervous System

Chapter V Case Studies   73
- Colored Plates and Sign Identification

IRIDOLOGY

Iridology is the science that uses the iris of the eye to diagnose and moniter tissue changes that are occurring or have occured within the body.

"The Doctor of the future will prescribe no drugs but will interest his patients in the care and nutrition of the human frame and in the cause and prevention of disease."

Thomas Edison

Dr. Donald Bamer, B.S., D.C.
Clinical Iridologist
Tulsa, Oklahoma

FOREWORD

This book has been written with both the public and the professional in mind. The average person should be able, after adequate study of the material contained herein, to identify healthy or unhealthy trends as they occur by monitoring the eye. By realizing the significance of these changes, if necessary, he can seek out a professional person who has had adequate training on the human body to help him return to a healthy state once again without the need of hospitalization or radical care. For the professional, this book supplies him with a non-invasive diagnostic tool to monitor the complete body of the patient at *one* time, applying his knowledge of the various body systems—endocrine, circulatory, neurological, etc., and correlate his examination findings. Thus enabling him to be able to detect the true cause of the patient's problems. It will also be explained how to monitor healing in the iris, along with suggested herbal remedies. In conjunction with this, specific charts of reflex points will be shown and explained for conjuctive treatment.

This book has further been written for the purpose of teaching and leading people to a holistic approach of health, treating the body not the symptoms.

The use of herbal remedies are recommended because of their purity and effectiveness.

The herbal recommendations and other treatment methods mentioned in this book are those that have been successfully used on patients in my Clinic or under my direction. These recommendations are not to be construed as a specific prescription for any specific person or problem. I have used the word "should" in the treatment section for the *Doctor* that might decide to follow my procedure exactly. If you feel you may have any of the conditions listed or described in this book, contact your Doctor, especially one who is a holistic practitioner and knowledgeable in this analytical procedure.

If you are unaware of this type of Doctor in your area, write or call:

NATIONAL IRIDOLOGY ASSOCIATION
3930 East 31st Street
Tulsa, Oklahoma 74135
(918) 742-9901

IRIS COLOR

The color of a person's eyes depends mainly upon his genetic configuration.

There are several theories about color and the number of basic colors. Some say there are but two basic colors; blue and brown, while others feel that hazel (a combination of both) should be included.

For the purpose of our studies it is more important to concern ourselves with the layers which are pigmented and iris *color changes* rather than the number of basic colors. As will be seen later, it is not uncommon for a patient that appears to have brown eyes, change eye color while undergoing treatment.

SPECIAL TERMINOLOGY OF ANATOMY
AS IT CORRELATES TO IRIDOLOGY

The collarette corresponds to the autonomic nerve wreath.

The sphincter pupillae corresponds to the stomach ring.

The Fuchs crypts corresponds to closed lesions.

The contraction furrows correspond to nerve rings/psychological stress rings/psychosomatic stress rings.

The neurasthenic ring is the pupillary pigment border.

The freckle or psoric spots are called Pigmented Nervi/Drug Spots/ Mineral Deposits/Pathological Poly Chromia.

The Wolffian bodies correspond to the lymphatic tophi.
psoric spots / sectoral hetechromia

CHAPTER 1
Introduction to Iridology

It has been said that the eyes are the windows to the soul, but within the last 150 years it has been realized that the eyes are also the windows to the body.

Indian medicine men have been known to sit and study the eyes of their patients for long periods of time before prescribing herbs or other remedies for their ailments.

Sheep herders would study the eyes of their sheep to tell when these animals were beginning to develop potential problems and need various remedies. One particular sign they looked for is an iris sign we call "Radii Solaris".

The Cauldeans are known to have studied and recorded changes in the irises of their friends and relatives as long ago as 3000 years; believing these changes to have an astronomical cause and significance.

Hippocrates was probably the first to realize that there was a definite link between signs in the eyes and changes in the body. He concentrated his efforts on the posterior aspect of the eye and established the beginning of what we use today as a basic ophthalmic exam.

Analysis of the posterior eye remained the significant area of examination up to the mid-eighteen hundreds. This began to change when a boy named Ignatz Peczely noticed that when an owl he was playing with became injured, a mark suddenly appeared in the iris of the owl's eye and on the same side of the injury. Thus was the discovery of a phenomenon we now call Ophthalmic-Somatic Analysis (Iridology).

Although completely unaware of the phenomenon he was observing, he remained very curious of his findings. This led him into medical school and eventually into a hospital in Budapest, where he furthered his knowledge in this new phenomenon. Here he was able to observe and examine all patients as they were admitted and discharged. Upon their admission, Dr. Peczely would study their case histories and their irises taking great efforts to draw in color, a picture of their irises and in exact detail. He would again draw a picture of their irises as they were released. He noticed that a pattern was developing and it was very consistent. As an example, when a person had a liver condition it always showed at eight o'clock in the right iris.

He was constantly being exposed to a large variety of patients and complaints, thus enabling him to begin forming a basic chart/map of the iris that corresponded to the location of organs and tissues. (See figure 1A.)

While continuing to improve and update this chart, he wrote the first book on Iridology, *Discovery in the Realm of Nature and the Art of Healing*. His book so excited the medical profession in Germany that they began writing about him and his discovery.

Some of the other great people in the historical development of Iridology were: Dr. Nils Liliquist, a Swedish Homeopath who worked with toxic appearances in the iris from vaccinations and was first to bring Iridology to America in the early 1900's, Dr. J. Haskell Kritzer, M. D. who wrote a text book, *Iris Diagnosis and Guide in Treatment*, Dr. Henry Lindlar, M. D., Chicago, and Dr. Henry Lahn, M. D., Austria. Each added significantly to the research and development of this phenomenon.

For many years what was taught in this Country was the information that was originally brought over by Dr. Liliquist and later up-dated, at least to the point of that time, by Dr. Lahn and Dr. Lindlar. However, in Germany a more indepth research program had begun and is still in progress today. This research began to discover the analytical significance of the whole eye and not just the iris. Their research included the retina, sclera and scleral vessels, iris, palpabrae, and even the cornuncle. For each of these structures has its individual story to tell. Their main significance is their correlative ability giving more than just one sign for a problem area. Because of the use of the whole eye, the Germans have renamed this science *"Opthalmic-Somatic Analysis"* instead of just iris analysis.

Ophthalmic-Somatic Analysis now became the key diagnostic science and as late as 1979 new research material was made available from which the most up-to-date Iridology chart now available has been produced. (See figure 2A.)

Just being able to identify a problem area is not enough. We must also know how to treat the patient's condition holistically with God given herbs and be capable of monitoring the healing through the eye.

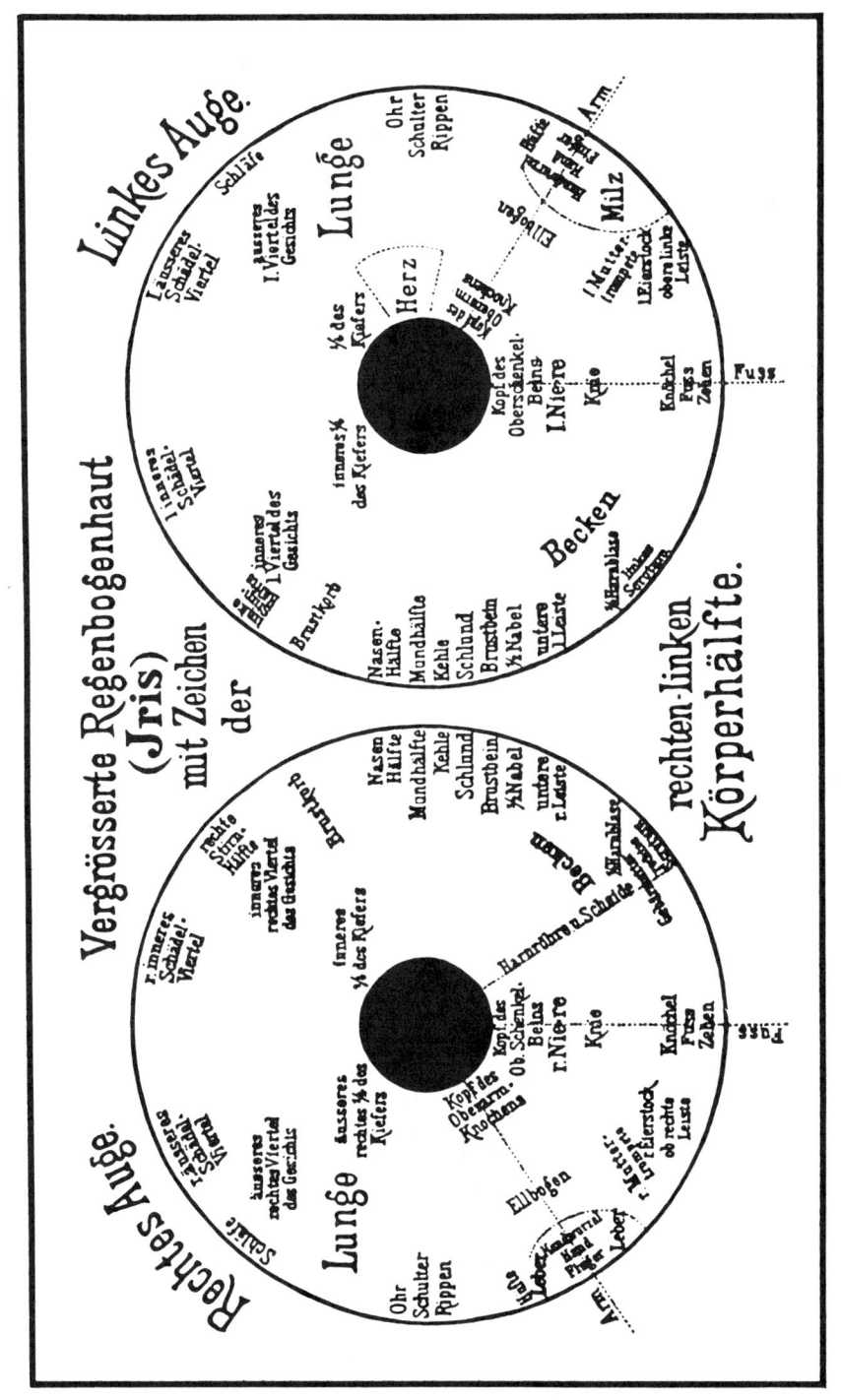

Fig. 1-A

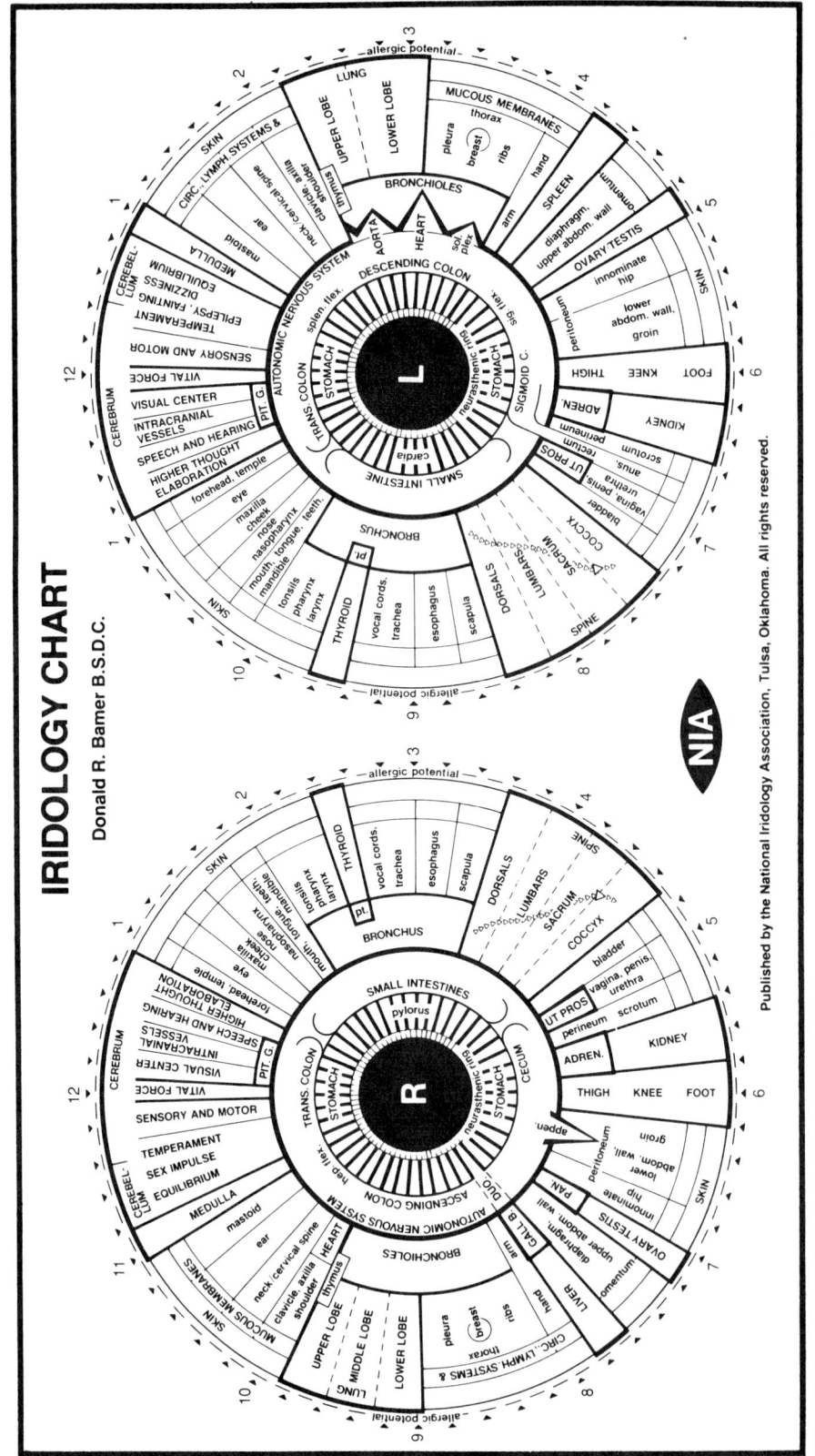

Fig. 2-A

HERBAL MEDICINES

Once an area has been identified as being in need of fortification, regardless for what reason, it is important to use something that will be effective and non-toxic at the same time. Often animal glandular products are used and are effective in many cases. But the true medicines that nature has provided for our use are the herbs. "And the fruit thereof shall be for meat and the leaf for medicine." (Ezekiel 47:12) Hippocrates, the Father of medicine, was an herbalist. He is recorded as saying that he could cure any of man's afflictions with just forty herbs. Hippocrates was the greatest healer the world has ever known. It is strange to think that he is the Father of modern medicine and yet has never given a patient a shot of penicillin, streptomyocin, or even an inorganic salve.

Herbs are effective because they are electromagnetically attracted to the organ or tissue they are known to effect. Once at the desired site, they supply the tissue with cellular nutrition complete with their own enzymes, co-enzymes, vitamins, minerals, trace substances, and anything and everything needed by the body which is able to use these products immediately to help the tissue restore normality.

The medicines used today are derivatives of medicinal plants, but because of man's greed and insistence upon playing the chemical game, these products now are synthetic and toxic to our bodies. Their purpose is to alleviate symptoms, not correct or cure any conditions. Herbal medicines, on the other hand, dispose of the symptoms by curing the condition. They restore normality and thus allow the body to regain homeostasis once again.

A prime example of the effectiveness of herbs can be seen by the example that the animal kingdom shows. An injured or sick animal will eat or otherwise use the herbs that will restore its health.

In many parts of the Orient, especially Okinawa, there is an over abundance of a large, long, thick snake the natives call a Habo. These Habos became so numerous that the Island Government began to import the famous mongoose—a natural enemy to poisonous snakes. The islanders will often put on display fights in the center of the village between the Habo and the mongoose. Once the fight starts it is not long until the mongoose has its teeth clenched in the back of the Habo's neck and from then on it is just a matter of time. Although there have been a few occasions where the Habo bit the mongoose, there is only one documented case of the mongoose dying from this bite, and that was because the animal was kept in captivity and not allowed to seek out the herbs that would save its life.

Previously, any time a mongoose had been bitten, it would seek out the herb "moss" and begin immediately rolling the area of the bite in the moss until the juice of the moss had an adequate chance to soak into the bitten area. The moss does several things. First, it acts as an astringent and causes localized vaso-constriction and stops the spread of the toxins. Second, it cleans and washes out the area. Third, it neutralizes the toxins, and fourth, it supplies large quantities of cellular nutrition at the site of injury, thus immensely enhancing the repair process.

During the years of my practice, I have used herbs in conjunction with spinal manipulation to treat and cure everything from "pink eye", blood poisoning, lupus erythematosis, complete blindness, to cancer almost anywhere on the body.

Herbs are potent yet very safe if used correctly. Before we go any further, I would like it made completely clear that I am not encouraging anyone to go into the fields, pick, and use any herbs for any reason. If there is ever a case of a person having a difficulty with herbs, it is usually because they have mistaken one herb for another. This can easily be done, so unless you have a Master's Degree in Botany and especially in herbal medicine, spend a few dollars and purchase the necessary pre-capsulated herbs from your doctor or local distributor.

I. How Iridology can help you.
   A. Iridology shows major and minor areas
      1. Inflammation
         a. Chronic
         b. Acute
      2. Poor elimination
      3. Acidity/Alkalinity
      4. Hypo-functioning organs
      5. Hyper-functioning organs
      6. Areas of ischemia
      7. Areas of enemia
      8. Underlying causes of symptoms
      9. Inherent weaknesses
      10. Acquired weaknesses
      11. Diverticulitis
      12. Vitamin and mineral dificiencies
      13. Poor assimilation

II. Anatomy and Neurology of the eye
    Motor
         1. Oculomoter, inferior and superior
            a. Superior branch
            b. Inferior branch
         2. Trochlear IV Cranial Nerve
         3. Abducens VI Cranial Nerve
    B. Autonomic nervous system
    C. Sympathetic innervation comes via the superior cervical ganglion
    D. Parasympathetic innervation comes via the third cranial nerve (Edinger-Westphal nucleus and ciliary ganglion)
    E. Both the sphincter and dilater muscles have a sympathetic and parasympathetic innervation

III. Blood Supply
    A. Ophthalmic Artery
       1. Origin: from internal coroted artery at the end of cavernous sinus
       2. Branches:
          a. In orbit to surrounding parts
          b. In orbit to eyeball
    B. Central Artery
       1. Eyeball
       2. Macula

Venous drainage of eyeball
1. Retina drained by veins that accompany branches and trunk of central arteries
2. Outer coats drained by vorticose veins in outer layer of choroid. These converge and drain into the superior ophthalmic vein.

IV. Accessory items of the anterior eye
   A. Sclera: The sclera/white of the eye is significant because of two reasons: (1) It is an area where much plaquing occurs, both yellow and white. These are secondary indications of lipid/cholesterol metabolic problems within the body. It often points to a liver dysfunction. (2) Scleral vessels are very significant as indicators pointing to a problem area in the body. There are vessels which indicate a back-pressure in the vascular system such as would be found with hemorrhoids.
   B. Palpabrae: The inferior palpabrae/eyelid often shows pigmentation changes such as liver spots when there is a liver dysfunction. This is a good confirmation test. The palpabrae, because of its rich blood supply, is an excellent area to detect systemic anemia. Under these conditions the palpabrae appears very white and bleached out.
   C. Pupillary response: The pupil is formed by two muscles, dilator pupillae and sphincter pupillae. The expansion and contraction of the pupil is an excellent way to evaluate the sphincter control throughout the whole body.
   The pupil is also a very good indicator of adrenal dysfunction. A wide pupil indicates adrenal weakness and possible exhaustion. A very tight pupil indicates hyper-adrenalism, thus over activity. This is a very significant sign because the adrenals are the glands of stress and play a major roll in common pathological conditions of today such as hypoglycemia and diabetes mellitus.
   D. Corununcle: The cornuncle, the little fatty ball nasal-ward in the corner of the eye, tends to attract much triglyceride and cholesterol plaquing and will begin showing signs often long before any other part of the anterior eye.

EYEBALL

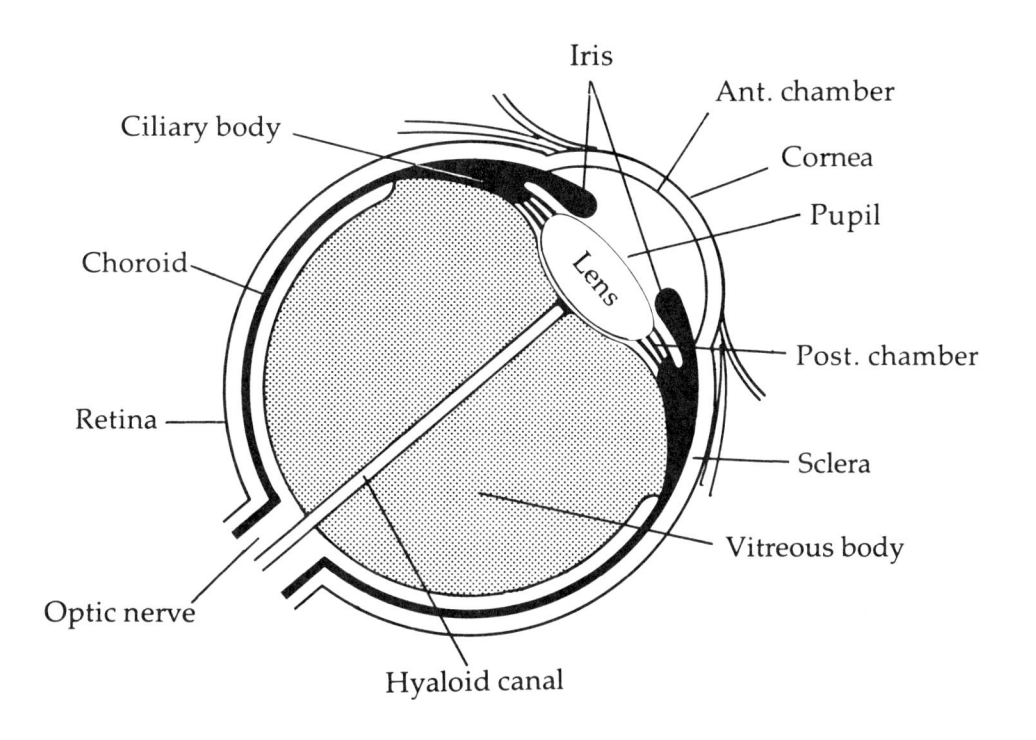

Fig. 3

IRIS LAYERS

The iris is composed of four separate layers, but only three are considered significant. They are from anterior to posterior.

1. Anterior border layer
   This layer is a modification of the middle stromal layer of the iris. It is composed of two layers: an anterior fibroblastic layer and a posterior pigmented layer. This posterior pigmented layer is the layer that has a great deal to do with the actual iris color.

2. Stromal layer

3. Posterior Epithelium layer
   It is the posterior ephithelium layer that is heavily pigmented with black and brown granules.

CHAPTER II
How this Phenomenon Works and Interpreting the Signs

How This Phenomenon Works

While in the maternal uterus, ophthalmic development begins from the frontal lobe of the brain. The eye, especially the iris, has a rich supply of neuro-ectodermal tissue. The iris has been estimated to contain over 28,000 individual nerve fibers mingled with stromal fibers. (This combination is extremely sensitive to nerve impulses from the automatic nervous system.) Since the brain is the ultimate control of the body, it must know (and does know) the complete condition of all organs and tissues of the body at all times. This is accomplished by constant flow of both afferent and efferent impulses to and from all parts of the body.

Certain neuron cells or aggregate of cells in the brain respond continuously to these impulses from the areas they control. These impulses are carried via the autonomic nervous system, both sympathetic and parasympathetic. This system feeds directly into the iris via the Edinger-Westphal nucleus (parasympathetic) and via the sympathetic ganglion in the upper thoracic spine. Since the iris has such a rich supply of highly sensitive neuro-ectodermal fibers, the iris functions like a remote T. V. picture tube, giving us a complete neurological picture of the body at all times by the reflex of neurological impulses. The significance of these impulses to the examiner is that they are at a frequency that corresponds to their health condition or any one of four stages of inflammation: acute, subacute, chronic, and degenerative.

Interpreting Iris Signs

The interpretation is done basically by noting two things:
1. A pigmentation change
2. A pattern change

AUTONOMIC NERVE SUPPLY OF EYE MUSCLES

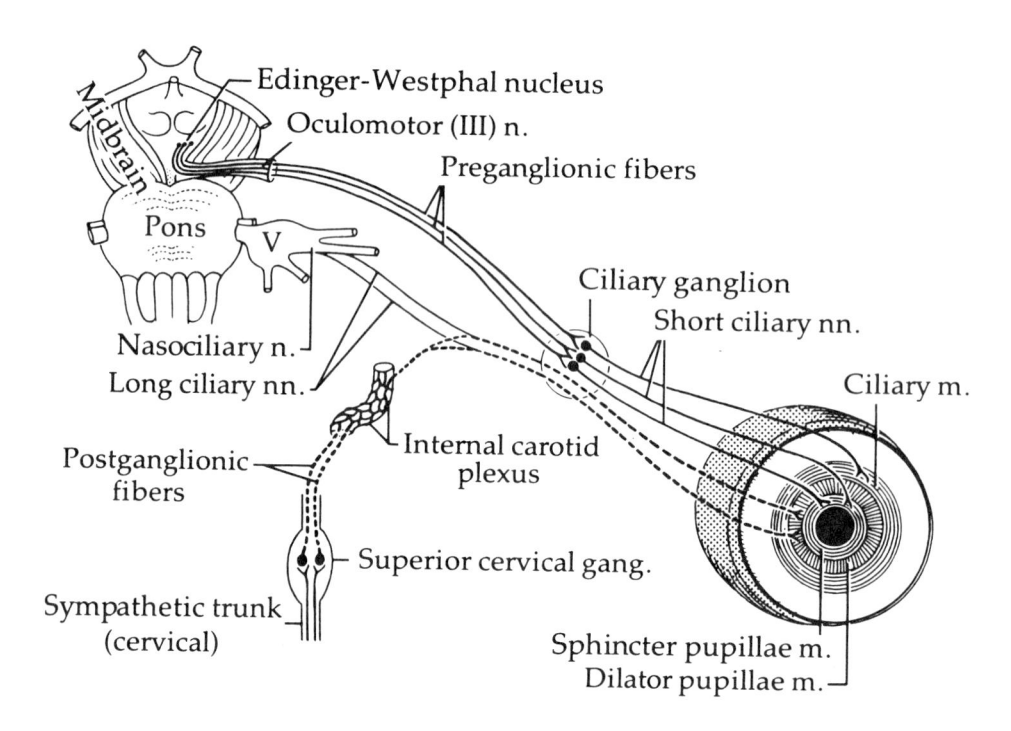

Fig. 4

The pigmentation changes correspond to stages of inflammation.
1. Acute—white
2. Subacute—light gray
3. Chronic—dark gray
4. Degenerative/Destructive—black

Acute inflammation (white) indicates in that area that there is increased activity which would be expected in any increased inflammation state, some of these being increased temperature, increased nerve function, and edema. These changes in this area cause the frequency of the nerve impulses going to the brain to be much higher than they would normally be. This change in frequency is being felt at the same time in the iris fibers. These fibers will also vibrate at a higher frequency which makes the area that they represent appear much whiter than adjacent areas.

A subacute (light gray) condition is very similar to acute but of a lesser degree. This iris fiber frequency is still elevated but not to the degree that it was in the acute condition.

A chronic (dark gray) condition requires our special attention for they are the underlying causes in most cases. For when a person has an acute condition, the body is responding and the patient is aware of the condition and the area of disturbance in most cases. But in the chronic state, these are the areas that the patient has either learned to live with or is operating at a subclinical level, as often is the case when the symptoms have been continuously suppressed through drug therapy. The area now is no longer performing its functions adequately, thus the whole body begins to feel the effect and accept some of the burden.

An example would be a chronic lung condition. Here the patient probably has no continuous problems, but more likely is very susceptible to bronchitis, pneumonia, etc. Yet this weakened pneumonic tissue now is no longer performing to its maximum abilities, one being oxygen/carbon dioxide exchange. Lack of adequate uptake of oxygen can lead to generalized hypoxia throughout the body. Also, more importantly, the lack of the lungs' ability to blow off carbon dioxide causes it to be changed in the body to carbonic acid, thus placing an additional burden on the kidneys. Even the cardiac activity will be directly affected by this change.

Some of the most common chronic problems found are those that are associated with hypoglycemia and diabetes mellitus. It is usually not the organs commonly suspected that are actually causing the problems, but instead a chronic or sluggish organ elsewhere which oftentimes eludes detection.

A destructive/degenerative (black) condition is the most serious sign that can be found in the iris. It indicates there is or has been destruction of the actual organ in that area, thus indicating a highly cancerous or precancerous condition. These should alert the examiner to request further lab work of a cancer screening nature immediately. These organs are placing a tremendous burden on the body because of their dysfunction.

These stages of inflammation correlate directly with the organ's activity. When an organ is in an acute inflammatory state, it is also overactive to that same degree and by the same token, underactive by the degree of chronicity indicated. Thereby these color changes allow us not only the ability to evaluate stages of inflammation, but also to be able to determine functional changes within the organs themselves.

Somatic Constitution
(Pattern Changes)

Since the fibers of the iris represent the structural soundness of any given area, we can use this to tell us the structural strength of any given area. We can evaluate it for possible inherent weaknesses, defect signs or other structural problems, or just as important, lack of problems.

Somatic constitution is set up in three categories:
1. Good. A good constitution is where the lines are straight and reasonably close together. This represents the body of a person with high recuperative capabilities. Once they begin to receive the proper care, they will bounce back very fast. There are virtually no significant weaknesses.
2. Fair. This person's iris fibers are not as close and tend to be fairly wavy. There is usually evidence of several lacuna (pockets) that will be discussed separately later in this book. Like the person with the good constitution, they tend to do fairly well when receiving the proper care, even though they have some inherent weaknesses.
3. Poor. The person with this type of constitution must work continuously to keep their bodies free from disease. Their fibers are widespread and there is multiple lacuna or crypts (pockets) in the iris indicating inherent weaknesses in these areas. These people also tend to be of the psychological nature that lack persistence and tend to give in easily. Oftentimes this type of person does not want to put forth any effort for

their health or even accept the responsibility for it. They will respond, but usually not 100%, and have to work very hard for all that they do get.

Finding the Zones

The iris develops neurologically from the pupil outward. There are a total of seven concentric zones. Each zone contains certain organs and tissues and acts as a rough guide in understanding the iris.

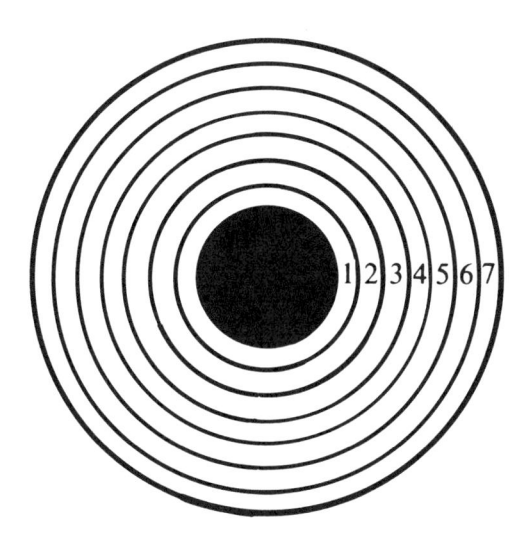

Fig. 6

Zone 1 Gastric mucosa
Zone 2 Complete intestinal tract, both small and large
Zone 3 Heart, pancreas, pituitary gland, adrenal glands, aorta, gall bladder, solar plexis, para thyroid, uterus/prostate pineal
Zone 4 Bronchial tubes
Zone 5 Brain and reproductive organs
Zone 6 Spleen, thyroid, liver, kidneys, and spine
Zone 7 This zone is lineated into a superior and inferior section. The inferior contains lymphatic and circulatory systems, motor and sensory nerves. The superior aspect reflects changes in the sweat glands and skin.

The Iris is laid-out neurologically like a clock

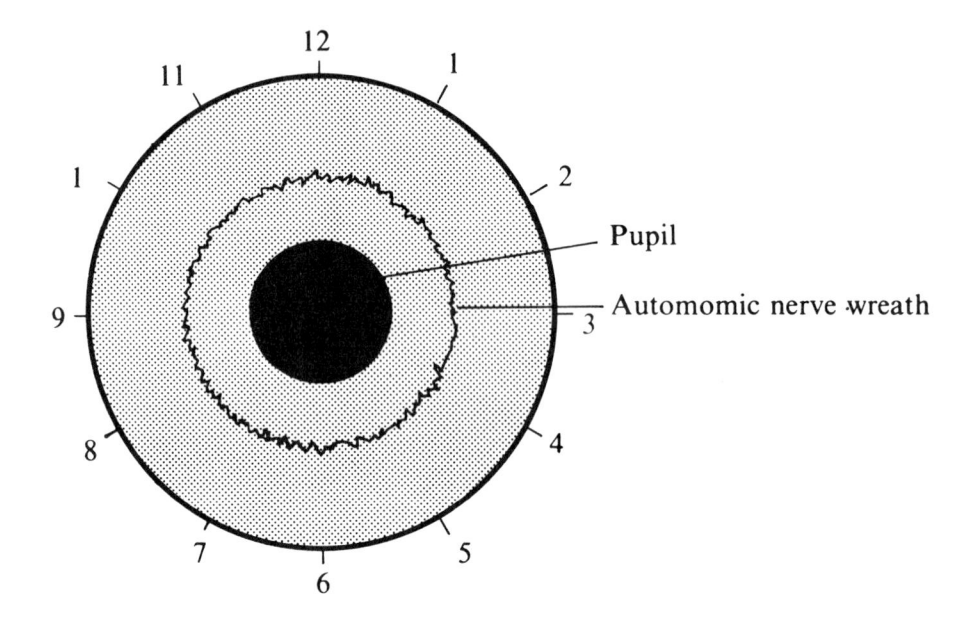

Fig. 5

ORGAN SIGNS

In addition to the irregular fibers and/or color changes in an area, research has identified several specific signs that are indications of inherited weaknesses. It was once thought in this Country that there were both inherited and acquired weaknesses, but research with thousands of people, especially families, show that all of the signs in the iris are inherited. In some cases they are not completely visible at a very young age but will be so by the time of growth completion for that particular area. Thus, all inherited signs usually appear by the age of six.

What we have found to be acquired is not a weakness of any particular area because we are what our parents are, at least physically. What we actually acquire is the health condition of that area and all areas of our bodies. The color in an area reflects how we have treated our bodies or an area of dysfunction—that is what is acquired. That is something we have control over and even though we cannot change a structural weakness that has formed, based upon its genetic blueprint, we can alter the color/health state of that or any other area of our body. Unless there has been an injury that has altered our structures, these signs should not be expected nor should the person be disapppointed if they do not disappear.

Leaf Lacuna: The leaf lucuna is commonly seen in the thoracic region of the iris. It is common with lung or heart weaknesses.

Open Lacuna: This is a very common sign and can be seen anywhere. In comparison to the leaf lacuna, the open lacuna indicates an area that is weaker.

Crypt: Although it can be seen anywhere, it is normally seen in the glandular zone. When several are seen and they are dark, this is an indication of a person having clinical manifestations of glandular problems such as diabetes mellitus, hypoglycemia, etc.

Open Crypt: Like the open lacuna it can be seen anywhere and has the same comparative value to the crypt as did the open lacuna to the leaf lacuna.

Kidney Medussa: Inherited kidney weakness will usually show with this sign. This sign, like the others, can be seen anywhere in the iris and wherever seen indicates an inherited weakness, but it is usually seen in the kidney zone.

The kidneys, like any of the organs of elimination, get constantly abused. They do not have to show a weakness to have dysfunction. These organs usually show a highly irritated state or a very chronic state, but if they are inherently weak also, this sign will be present.

ORGAN SIGNS

LEAF LACUNA

OPEN LACUNA

CRYPT

OPEN CRYPT

HONEY COMB

KIDNEY MEDUSSA

LIVER STAKE

DEFECT SIGN

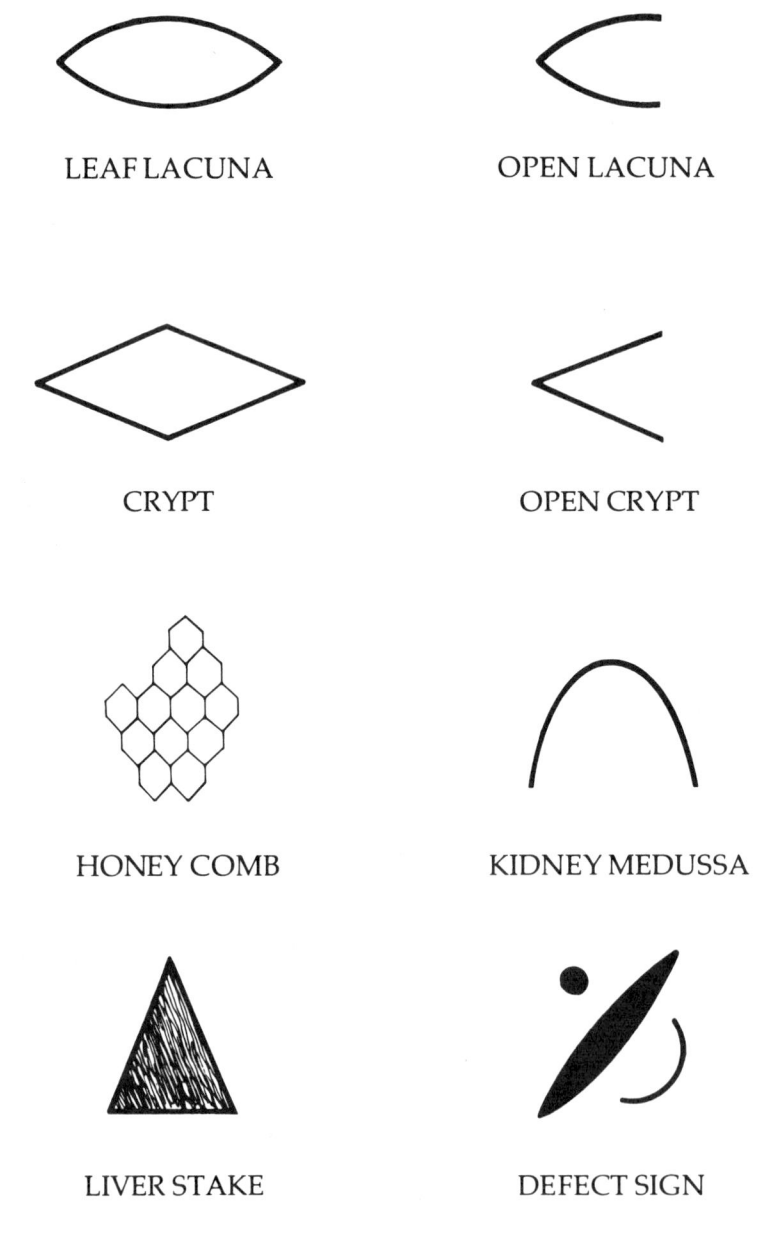

Fig. 7

Liver Stake: This is the sign most often seen in the liver zone when there is an inherited weakness present. The base of the triangle is on the outside of the iris and the tip points towards the pupil.

Defect Signs: This sign is not made of the combination of these: ● dot, ✐ spearhead,) and comma or fish hook. But only one will be seen in any particular area. They are normally seen very near an inherited weakness. They are tar black in color and signify an area that is more than just weak but in fact, an area that if allowed to become chronic, is very susceptible to becoming cancerous much faster than adjacent areas. Thus the name *defect* requires much more attention than just a weakened area.

Honey Comb: This sign has very significant meanings. It is not an inherited weakness but an indication of a functional problem of metabolism occurring at that location. This sign has possibilities of diminishing as the problem is corrected.

CHAPTER III
Significant Iridology Findings

PUPILLARY CHANGES

The pupil is an opening in the eye that sits medial-nasalward in the eye. Its purpose is to allow light into the eye. These impressions excit the optic nerve and from this we have vision.

The pupil also contracts to close-out light and to focus on close objects. This contraction is accomplished by the action of a muscle surrounding the pupil named "Sphincster Pupillae".

The pupil expands to allow more light in and to focus on objects further away. This expansion/dilation of the pupil is accomplished by the "Dilator Pupillae".

Both of these muscles are under direct control of the autonomic nervous system, parasympathetic, and sympathetic. Whenever there is pressure on the nerve root such as in the case with a spinal subluxation, the pupil will flatten across from the area serviced by that nerve supply. An example is if there is nerve root pressure in the upper thoracic spine, the pupil will flatten on the side of the greatest interference and across from the lund and upper respiratory region on the Iridology Chart. Thus the pupil tells us where there is nerve interference and which areas it is affecting. It is also corrected very quickly once the interference has been removed. So it further provides us with feedback for the correction of nerve root pressure.

The lining of the pupil has been found to be very helpful in detecting metabolic and pathological problems. The pupillary lining has been noted as becoming very irregular when the patient is having a glucose tolerance problem, especially diabetes mellitus. A urinalysis and glucose screening test should be accomplished on all of these patients.

STOMACH, HYPO-ACTIVE

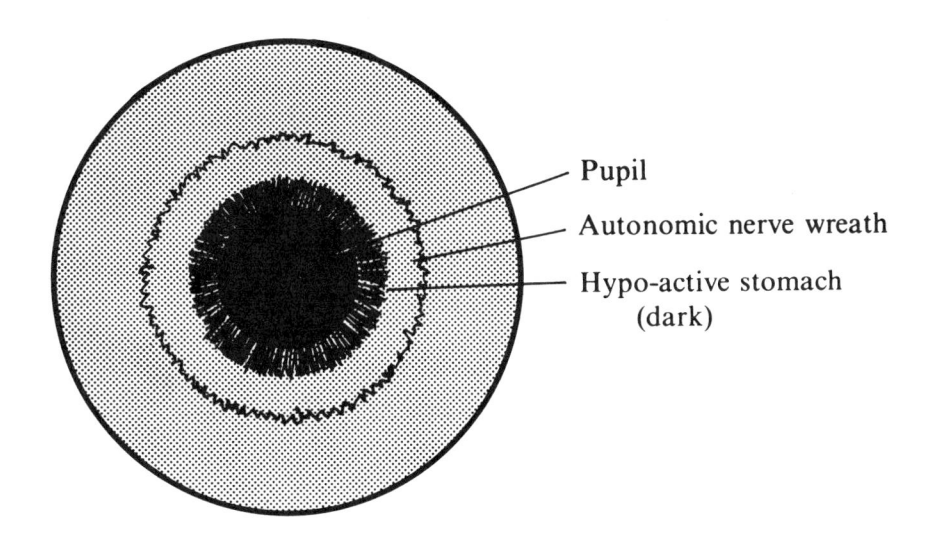

- Pupil
- Autonomic nerve wreath
- Hypo-active stomach (dark)

A hypo-active/under active stomach is probably one of the most subtle causes of malnutrition known to man. When this condition exists, there is a dark ring around the pupil in the stomach zone of the iris. This ring is called the "stomach ring" and whenever seen, indicates gastric/stomach dysfunction. If the ring is white, the dysfunction is one of over activity and if dark, is one of *under* activity. Most people with under active stomachs are unaware of any stomach problem.

Some common symptoms are: easy nausia, frequent belching and burping after meals, stomach and bowel gas, and a general feeling of weakness. These people are suffering from malnutrition because their foods are not being broken down adequately and thus not absorbed. Many people will report finding their vitamins, especially minerals, and even complete food particles in their stool upon the completion of a bowel movement.

Whenever treating anyone nutritionally, this area must be evaluated and worked with if any results are to be expected at all. Remember, it is not what you eat, but what you assimilate that counts.

Treatment Considerations

A combination of comfrey papain or comfrey pepsin taken one

half hour before meals does very well in aiding proper digestion. The very chronic stomach may require two capsules before each meal while the mild case usually requires only one before each meal.

A combination of papaya/mint is very effective in combating indigestion.

STOMACH-HYPER ACTIVE

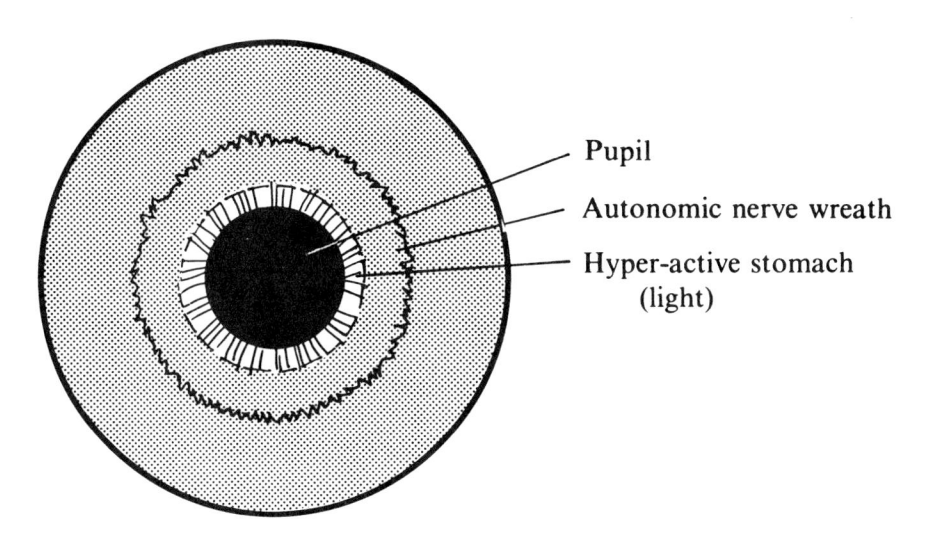

- Pupil
- Autonomic nerve wreath
- Hyper-active stomach (light)

When the stomach is hyper-active, whether acidic or alkaline, it will show as a white ring around the pupil. This ring being named, and rightfully so, a "stomach ring". Some of the symptoms that can be associated with this sign is heartburn, sensitivity to such items as coffee, tea, alcohol, tobacco, citrus fruits, and spices. In very severe cases patients have been known to actually spit-up the excessive digestive acids.

The most common pathology associated with this condition is ulceration. They can be located in either the gastric mucosa or the duodenum/small intestine.

Treatment Considerations

The most effective treatment for this condition is a combination of specific spinal treatments such as would be expected from a Chiropractor or Osteopath and one to two Tablespoons of Aloe Vera liquid fifteen minutes before each meal and one half teaspoon of Cayenne Tincture in warm distilled water.

Cayenne is one of the greatest healers known to man. Even though hot and used in many cases as a pepper, Cayenne, if taken correctly, can heal a bleeding ulcer almost completely within 48 hours.

A combination of Golden Seal, capsicum, and myrrh gum is often used in the Cayenne Tincture for a very sensitive stomach.

TOXIC COLON

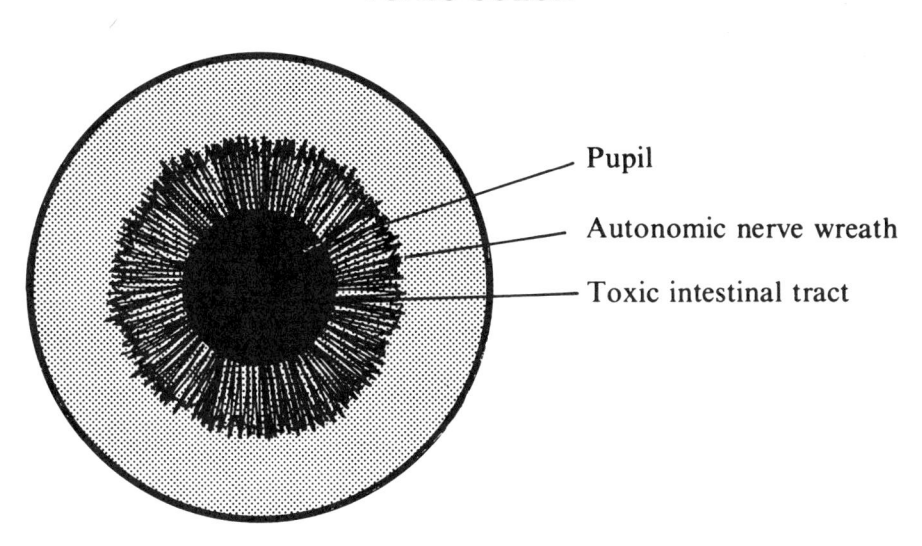

- Pupil
- Autonomic nerve wreath
- Toxic intestinal tract

The colon easily becomes toxic because of its function in disposing of body wastes. This waste material often remains in the large intestine for months and even years, decaying more and more, producing poisons, and seaping into the body through the bowel wall. Most of this seapage is gradual except in the case where a radii solaris or radial furrow sign is present.

Most people in this Country do not have a normal bowel movement or even know what a normal bowel movement is. Any person eating three "normal" sized meals per day should have one or two good bowel movements *per day*. Anyone eating more than this should have an appropriate increase. Anything less that this is allowing this material to remain in the body, decay, and produce large amounts of poisons that will find their way into the blood stream. The colon often begins to balloon out and causes what is called "diverticuli" or pockets in the bowel wall.

Treatment Considerations

There are two excellent herbal formulas on the market that work to rebuild muscle strength of the intestinal wall, step-up intestinal elimination, break down these pockets, and even feed the nerves associated with the parastaltic activity necessary for elimination. The first formula consists of: Cascara Sagrada Bark,

Barberry Bark, Cayenne, Ginger, Golden Seal Root, Lobelia, Red Raspberry Leaves, Turkey Rhubarb Root, and Fennel.

The second formula consists of: Cascara Sagrada Bark, Buckthorn Bark, Licorice Root, Capsicum Fruit, Ginger Root Barberry Root Bark, Couchgrass Herb, Redclover Tops and Lobelia Herb.

When using any bowel cleanser it is very important never to induce diarrhea.

RADII SOLARIS
(Radials from the Sun)

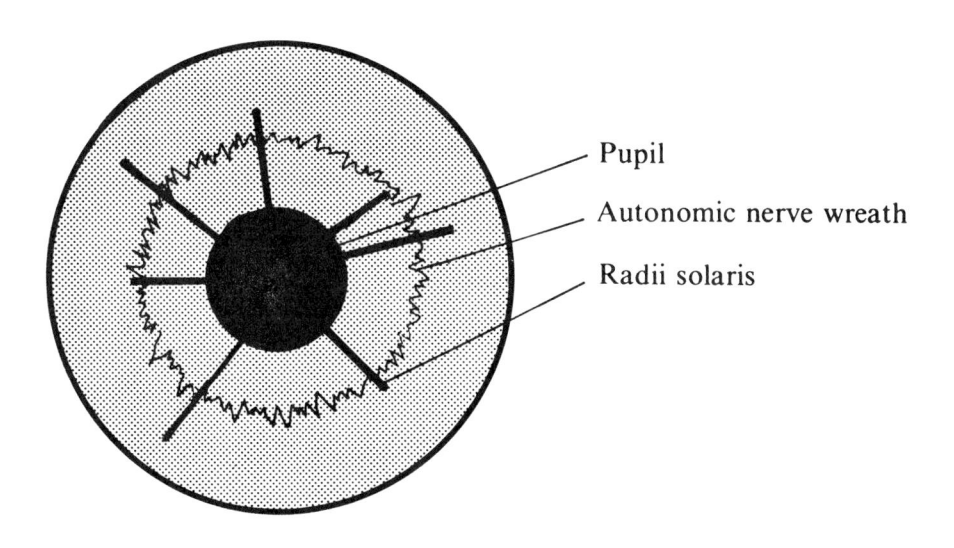

- Pupil
- Autonomic nerve wreath
- Radii solaris

This sign is probably one of the oldest ever identified. Its use has been extremely widespread. It has been used traditionally by the many herders to maintain the health of their herds; detecting a problem prior to the manifestation of symptoms. This sign gets its name because it appears as radials from a central object—the pupil. Each of these radials indicates a low level of seapage from the intestinal tract into that area represented on the chart. Thus producing a low level of septasemia (septic blood) and inflammation. This area may be high in parasite activity. The prevelance of parasites in the United States is extremely high. Estimates to be at least 90%. Most pathologists will agree that during most autopsies they find an extremely high rate of parasites. This sign is also very special because it causes a reflexed irritation of the nervous system at the level it is seen, plus directly affects the adjacent tissue (adjacent on the iris chart). With this sign the colon and other areas of the G. I. tract have a general and constant leakage of toxic material. This material goes directly into the blood. This sign indicates more than just routing seapage, it is as though a trough has been dug right through the intestine wall into the adjacent tissue. Thus allowing toxic material into these areas at a very fast rate.

Treatment Considerations

The bowel wall must be repaired and the musculature strengthened. The best herbal formula for this is one of Cascara Sagrada Bark, Barberry Bark, Cayenne, Ginger, Golden Seal Root, Lobelia, Red Respberry Leaves, Turkey Rhubarb Root, and Fennel. A dosage of one three times a day should be used as a starter and then increased up to a point of just prior to diarrhea. Once the patient has begun a good elimination program for at least seven days, they should then begin an abdominal exercise that will help strengthen both the abdominal musculature and the muscles surrounding the intestinal tract. Although this will help cleanse the areas where the parasites tend to multiply it will not kill them. For parasitic control a marvelous formula is Pumpkin Seed, Culver's Root, May Apple, Violet Leaves, Poke Root, Cascara Sagrada, Witch Hazel Bark, Mullein, Comfrey Root, and Slippery Elm Bark. This formula can be taken two capsules per day for six days, off two days, and then taken again for 6 days. The patient should wait two weeks and begin the program again.

RADIAL FURROWS

- Pupil
- Autonomic nerve wreath
- Radial furrows

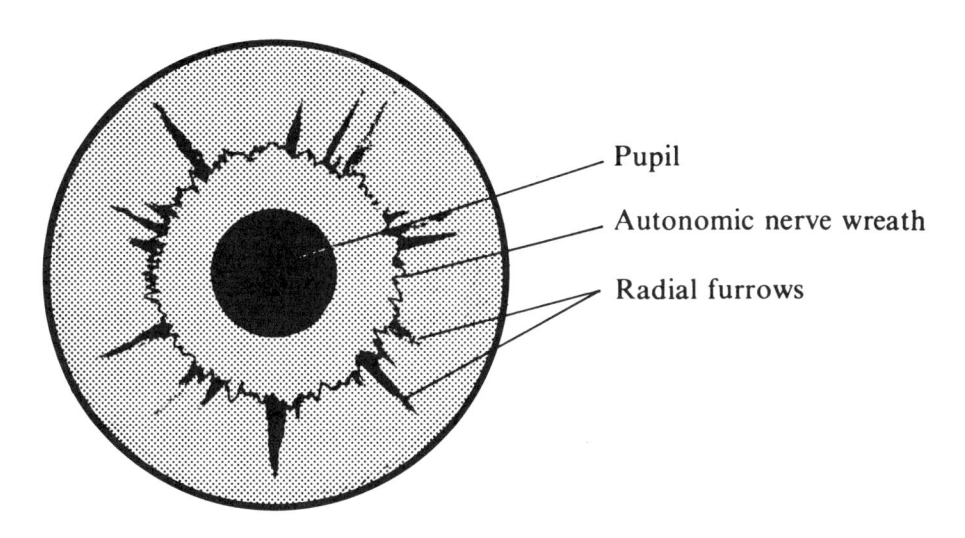

Like the radii solaris, this sign indicates increased toxic material in the adjacent and surrounding tissue. However, one big difference in recognizing this condition is that unlike the radii solaris, the radial furrow is always found outside the autonomic nerve wreath.

This condition is more severe than just a toxic colon but less severe than a radii solaris. Knowing these three different stages of toxicity of the intestinal tract enables us to evaluate the progress and stage of this condition.

Treatment Considerations

This condition responds to the same herbal combination as the radii solaris. The bowel wall must be repaired and the musculature strengthened. The best herbal formula for this is one of Cascara Sagrada Bark, Barberry Bark, Cayenne, Ginger, Golden Seal Root, Lobelia, Red Raspberry Leaves, Turkey Rhubarb Root, and Fennel. A dosage of one three times a day should be used as a starter and then increased up to a point of just prior to diarrhea. Another herbal formula which has been used very successfully is one of: Gentian, Catnip, Golden Seal, May Apple, Barberry Bark, Myrrh Gum, Yellow Dock, Comfrey, Irish Moss, Fenugreek, Pink Root, Chickweed Black Walnut, Dandelion, Safflowers, St. Johnswort, Echinacea, Poke Root, Cyani Flowers. Once the patient has begun a good elimination program for at least seven days, they should then begin an abdominal exercise that will help strengthen both the abdominal musculature and the muscles surrounding the intestinal tract.

PARASITES

Parasites are extremely common in this Country. Anyone who has ever had a pet, a child, or both, probably at one time or another has contacted parasites. These can range from pin worms to tape worms and everything in between.

People with diverticuli in their intestinal tracts and especially radii solaris and radial furrows can be expected to have quite an abundance of parasites.

I might mention here that these parasites do not remain within the intestinal tract only, but have been found in all parts of the body, even the brain. Travel becomes very easy for them once a canal between the bowel and the circulatory system has been provided, as is the case with radii solaris.

Pathological problems from parasites are endless. They can and often are the underlying cause of conditions such as Lupus Erythematosus, Multiple Sclerosis, and many more.

Treatment Considerations

For parasitic control a marvelous formula is Pumpkin Seed, Culver's Root, May Apple, Violet Leaves, Poke Root, Cascara Sagrada, Witch Hazel Bark, Mullein, Comfrey Root, and Slippery Elm Bark. This formula can be taken two capsules three times a day for six days, off two days, and then taken again for six days. The patient should wait two weeks and begin the program again.

Before a person begins a strong parasitic purge they should first insure that they have been having at least 2-3 very good bowel movements for at least 7-10 days. Use of the bowel cleansing formulas plus Black Walnut as a single herb will accomplish the cleanse.

Exercise that enables the person to move up and down such as on a home (mini-trampoline) exercisor is excellant in assisting any eliminative problem.

DIVERTICULI

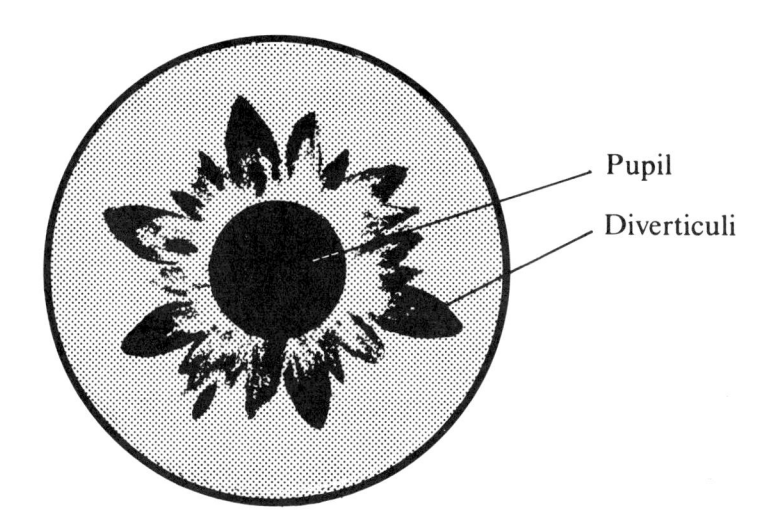

Pupil
Diverticuli

Bowel pockets are formed either because of a pre-exisiting weakness in that area or because the large intestine is so full of waste material that the bowel was forced to balloon out. These areas become full of waste material and become a breeding ground for harmful bacteria and parasites. These areas further create a constant irritation to the bowel wall in that area and are often the precursor to cancer of the colon, a form of cancer very high in this country.

Treatment Considerations
The herbal compositions suggested for the toxic colon are also very effective on this condition as well. These compositions being: Cascara Sagrada Bark, Barberry Bark, Cayenne, Ginger, Golden Seal Root, Lobelia, Red Raspberry Leaves, Turkey Rhubarb Root, Fennel.

Cascara Sagrada Bark, Buckthorn Bark, Licorice Root, Capsicum Fruit, Ginger Root, Barberry Root Bark, Couch Grass Herb, Red Clover Tops and Lobelia Herb.

Because herbs are food, they cannot be taken excessively. However, it is necessary to use a little common sense. Any type of prolonged diarrhea should never be allowed.

AUTONOMIC NERVE WREATH

The autonomic nerve wreath is the only structure seen in the iris that is normal. All her structures; color changes, etc., are indications of an abnormal condition.

The autonomic nerve wreath is also significant as a landmark. It surrounds the gastro-intestinal tract and gives us an outline of the stomach, small intestines and large intestines at all times. This is significant because when the bowel wall balloons out, such as with hypo-toxicity, we are able to see at exactly what location this has occurred. The autonomic nerve wreath further gives us the indication of a prolapsed and even a spastic colon because of its (the wreath's) location.

This wreath as a landmark separates what is in the intestinal tract and what is not. That way we can tell if an organ is directly involved or indirectly involved by reflexed action. Knowing this adds to our success and accuracy in analysis.

The wreath also is a direct indication of one of the most important systems of the body—the autonomic nervous system. It is this system that the brain uses to control the body.

The autonomic nervous system can be thought of as an automatic system in that it controls the digesting of our food, our vision, and controls circulation. The list is endless.

The color of the wreath is significant because it gives us indications of the condition of the system. As an example, if it is very white, it indicates that it is highly irritated.

Interruption of the wreath indicates a lack of adequate nerve supply in the area of the interruption.

Irritation of the atuonomic nervous system, such as often found from the intestinal tract, can and does reflex nerve action into other, often remote, areas of the body. There are special reflexed indications when this occurs. These will be discussed at a later time.

Treatment Considerations

Those which show disturbances in the autonomic nervous system should have a complete spinal and neurological examination. The purpose of which is to locate any and all areas of nerve root pressure.

They should also begin taking high levels of Brewer's Yeast, or preferable a Rice bran syrup; 1 Tablespoon three times a day. This syrup is extremely high in niacin and the other B complexes. A patient deficient in niacin will tend to flush-up for a varying degree of time, depending upon the degree of their deficiency. This flushness or rash should be completely dissipated within four to six hours. As the deficiency is corrected, there will be less and less reaction to the niacin.

When Rice Bran syrup is not available a natural source of B-complex tablets may be taken. Most adults require 1-2 tablets 3 times a day while this condition is being treated.

There are two herbal formulas that are very good for the autonomic nervous system. They not only soothe the nerves, but they also build-up the nerve sheath. The first of these being a combination of Black Cohosh, Cayenne, Hops Flowers, Misteltoe, Lobelia, Scullcap, Wood Betony, Lady's Slipper, and Valerian Root. This can be taken two three times a day.

The second combination is Horsetail Grass, Oat Straw, Comfrey, and Lobelia. This formula will aid the first one and also provide the body with many minerals, calcium being but one.

PROLAPSED COLON

— Prolapsed colon
— Pupil

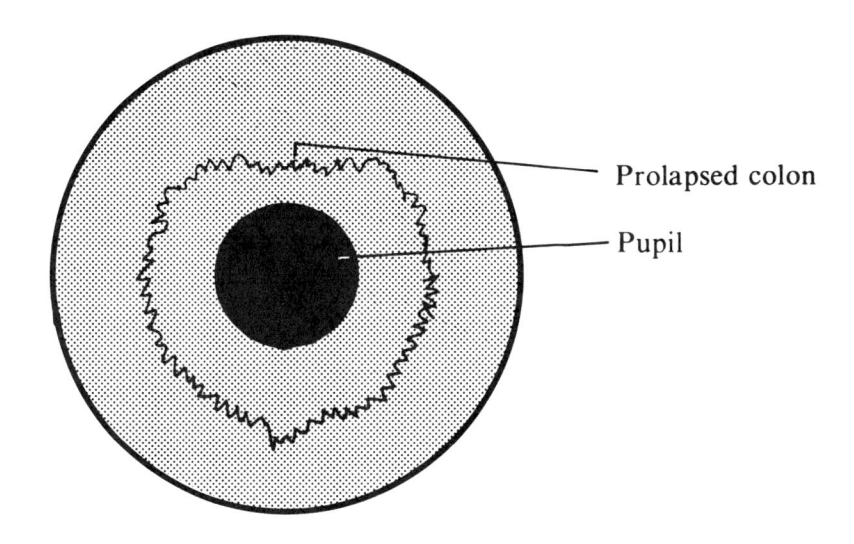

The transverse colon, because of its size and position, is often the underlying cause of many conditions, especially in those who have allowed their abdominal area to become very large. The prolapse can be detected by the flatness of the autonomic nerve wreath and by its closeness to the pupil.

The transverse colon cause most of its problems by exerting physical pressure on the organs of the pelvic cavity; bladder, prostate, uterus, vagina, etc. There is basically four reasons for this pressure: (1) Very weak musculature of the intestinal wall, allowing the transverse colon to sag and lie upon the organs, (2) the transverse colon becomes impacted with fecal matter because of a history of constipation, and down it goes. (3) Another common cause, but one that is often overlooked, is nerve interference in the lumbar spine and thus to the large intestine. Because the nerve supply to the tendons and musculature of the transverse colon is being interrupted, it also removes the supply for ligamentous tonus. The transverse again is allowed to sag and the end result is the same as previously described. (4) The fourth and very common cause, among women especially in this Country, is a hysterectomy. After women have this surgery it leaves a certain degree of emptiness in the pelvic cavity thus encouraging protrusion of the transverse colon into that area.

Treatment Considerations

Abdominal exercises are very important, especially those that do not stress the lumbar spine such as leg lowering. Spinal adjustments are necessary to increase the tone of the colon ligaments, tendons, and musculature.

The patient should use a slant board, the patient should massage the pelvic organs and work them towards the head. The slant board reverses the gravitational effects on the body and is extremely beneficial for anyone who does prolonged standing.

Daily exercise on a home rebounder type of exerciser is a must for these people. At least 5 minutes twice a day.

A very good herbal composition is one of Lobelia, Mullein, Black Walnut Leaves, Marshmallow Root, Yellow Dock Root, White Oak Bark, and Comfrey Root. This formula can usually be obtained in both bulk and capsule form. It should be taken both orally and as a douche. A capsule dosage varies with the condition, but two three times a day is usually found to be satisfactory. As a tea use one Tablespoon three times a day in 8 oz. of distilled water. The water should be just under boiling temperature. The tea is added, stirred several times, and allowed to steep for ten minutes, strain, then drink the tea while it is still hot. Peppermint tea or honey may always be added to enhance the flavor.

Another very good combination is: Squaw Vine, Chickweed, Slippery Elm, Comfrey, Yellow Dock, Golden Seal, Mullein, Marshmallow.

Rosehips in large amounts (3-4 4 times daily) should also be taken because of its ability to build and repair torn ligaments and tendons.

As a douche it should be made into a tea, strained, and inserted vaginally while still warm. The women should be either on a slant board or in a position to allow maximum retention. The men need to be in the same position and insert the tea rectally. This procedure is most effective when done two times a day for thirty days.

INCREASED TISSUE ACIDITY

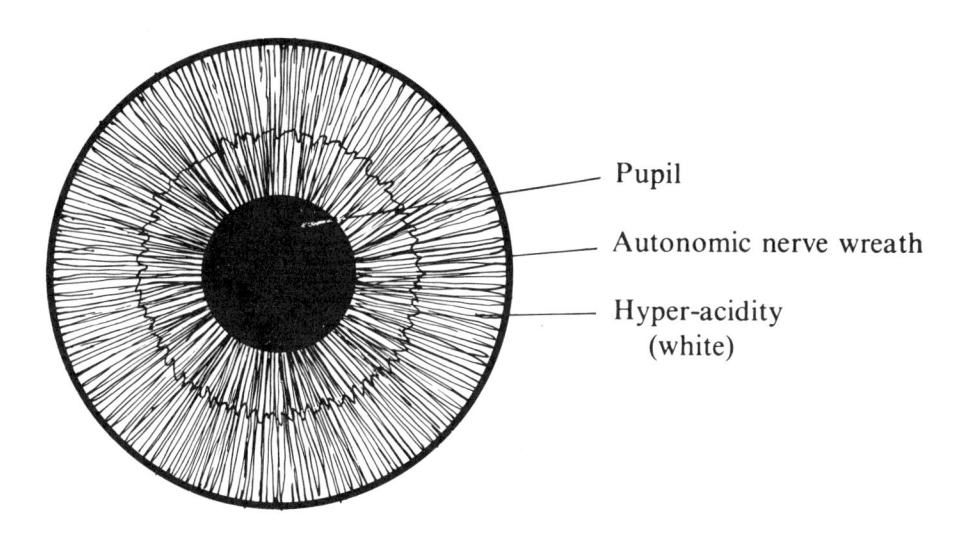

- Pupil
- Autonomic nerve wreath
- Hyper-acidity (white)

This is probably the most common problem found today, especially among the younger generation. There are several major causes. (1) The end product of metabolism is CO_2 and water. Thus almost everything we eat ends up as acid in the body. (2) Simple carbohydrates/sugars are extremely acid forming foods as well as meats, coffee, tea, alcohol, spices, and even citric acid fruits such as lemons, oranges, and grapefruit. One might say they thought these citric acid fruits were actually alkaline in nature. They are, but that is only when they have been completely vine-ripened. These Super Market fruits, tomatoes included, are extremely acid forming because they have not had a proper gestation period. This highly acidic condition places a very large demand upon the body to be neutralized. The body primarily uses sodium to neutralize this acidic condition. Most people in this Country are extremely deficient in a natural sodium. This does not mean table salt, but the sodium that is obtained from foods such as kelp, celery, parsley, etc. Because of this deficiency, the body is forced to draw upon its storehouse of this mineral. Sodium is stored primarily in two places, the stomach and the joints.

The stomach is usually the first area to give-up its supply of this precious mineral, thus encouraging an "acid stomach" and the usual needs for an anti-acid. This may be the beginning of a gastric ulcer.

Now the body begins to give-up more and more sodium from the joints, these joints begin to become infiltrated by calcium and become rigid, very irritated, and inflamed. Thus the real importance of the sign "high Acidic Tissue" is it is the underlying cause of much of the arthritis today, especially rheumatoid—the crippler.

Treatment Considerations

These people should be placed on very low acidic diets. This means to avoid the high acidic foods previously mentioned and above all, no red meat or pork. They can have all the fish or fowl they desire. They should remain off these foods completely for thirty days. After thirty days, they will normally begin feeling so good that if they begin eating these foods again, they quickly notice the difference. This is usually convincing enough evidence for them to continue to avoid these products.

Several formulas have been very successful. A combination that both increases the natural minerals and helps the body neutralize the existing condition is one that contains Parsley, Watercress, Kelp, Irish Moss, Romaine Lettuce, Turnip Tops, and Iceland Moss. Very large dosages such as four six times a day usually brings fast results.

Another excellant formula is: Yucca, Bromalin Powder, Alfalfa, Comfrey, Black Cohosh, Chaparral, Burdock, Poke Berries, Yarrow, Cayenne, Centaury, Lobelia.

This formula is often found in a concentrated form and should be used concentrated in severe cases. Yucca as a single herb is used as a booster. Vitamin C in the Rose Hips form (3-4 times daily) is also helpful for its anti toxic and anti bacterial effects.

HYPER-ALKALINE TISSUES

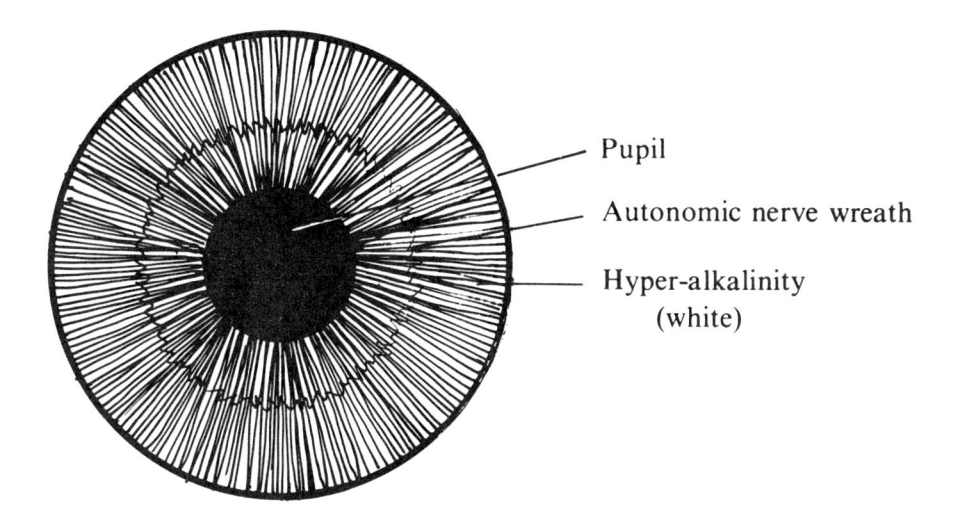

- Pupil
- Autonomic nerve wreath
- Hyper-alkalinity (white)

Like hyper-acidity, this is an abnormal condition within the tissues. We tend to think of acidity as always being bad and alkalinity as always being good. This is not the case. Once the PH of an area begins to go either acid or alkaline, there is going to be trouble and much in the same manner. They are just horses of a different color. DRAIN—O, the highly active substance that is often used in drains and sinks will burn the skin severely if contact is made. DRAIN—O is an *alkaline* not an *acid*.

The build-up of this alkalinity in the body cells and tissues prevents the cells from adequately disposing of its waste material and likewise causes an inadequacy of taking on the desperately needed nutrition from the blood.

Hyper-alkalinity is normally found in people in their 30's and up who have had a history of ulcers or an acid stomach. Most of this build-up comes from ingesting high quantities of anti-acids such as Rolaids, Tums, Alka-Seltzers, white flour products, baking soda and similar products.

This high alkalinity is usually of sodium, but of the inorganic type. Sodium displaces potassium in the system. Potassium is crucial for normal nerve function and brain function. Also potassium is needed in the muscles, especially in the caridac muscle.

Potassium is stored in the intestinal tract and gets depleted under a condition of diarrhea. It is not uncommon for an elderly person to die from a heart attack after a long bout of diarrhea.

If there is any question as to whether the patient is suffering from a hyper-acidic or a hyper-alkaline condition, hair analysis will usually show whether there is a high amount of sodium or potassium condition.

Treatment Considerations

These people need to avoid salt and all other sources of inorganic sodium, including diet foods or drinks. Their body has a demand for sodium, but of the natural sodium such as found in kelp, alfalfa, parsley, celery, etc. They should be on foods high in potassium such as bananas (provided they can be obtained vine ripe).

Herbal considerations are Elderberry Tincture or Syrup. This is an extremely high source of potassium. Other good sources are Kelp or Alfalfa. These can be taken three times a day. A very good combination is: Juniper Berries, Parsley, Ura Ursi, Marshmallow, Lobelia, Ginger, and Golden Seal Root. This can be taken four, three times a day. This is also a very good formula for any kidney infection or weakness.

Another very effective herbal combination is: Ura Ursi, Parsley, dandelion, Juniper Berries and Chamomile.

Herbal potassium should also be used 2-3 times daily.

PSYCHOSOMATIC STRESS RINGS

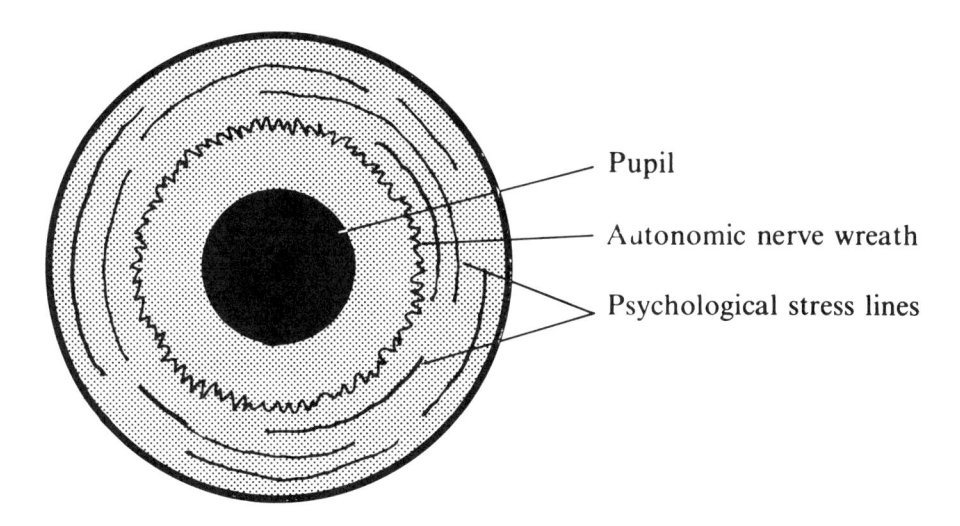

- Pupil
- Autonomic nerve wreath
- Psychological stress lines

This is a very common but significant sign. These rings can be complete or partial and there can be one or more rings. They signify a person whose body is under a lot of stress. This stress can either be from a psychological or physical origin. These rings also are indicative of organs and tissue under a neurological stress, probably because they also indicate a calcium deficiency which is effecting the nerve sheath in that area. This indication of a calcium deficiency receives more comment from patients than any other sign, especially from a person that is on a high calcium diet. It is not what you take that counts, but how well your body uses what is taken. Almost without fail, these people have abnormal gastrointestinal activity. This attributes highly to their deficiency because of poor absorption. Calcium is one of the hardest supplements to be broken down by the body. If the digestive system is not working almost perfectly, the calcium supplements will only be partially broken down and from that time on is treated as a synthetic by the body. This could lead to both placquing and kidney stones. But this will *always* lead to a nutritional deficiency of calcium.

The severity of this condition can be estimated by the number of these lines, how much tissue they go through and how deeply they are entrenched. These will usually go away very slowly depending upon how long the patient had them and the above mentioned considerations.

Treatment Considerations

I find that these people repond very well to herbs and tea high in horsetail grass and alfalfa. Also a combination that contains Valerian Voot and Wild Lettuce works very well. A high B Complex is necessary.

Specific herbal formulas for this condition are: capsicum, Valerian Root, Black Cohosh, Mistletoe, Ginger, Hops, Wood Betony, St. Johnswort.

or:

Black Cohosh, Capsicum, Hops, Mistletoe, Lobelia, Scullcap, Wood Betony, Lady's Slipper, Valerian Root, Rosehips (2-3 times daily) is very beneficial as an anti stress agent.

Valerian Root and Horsetail Grass are often used as single herbs to boost in conjunction with a combination.

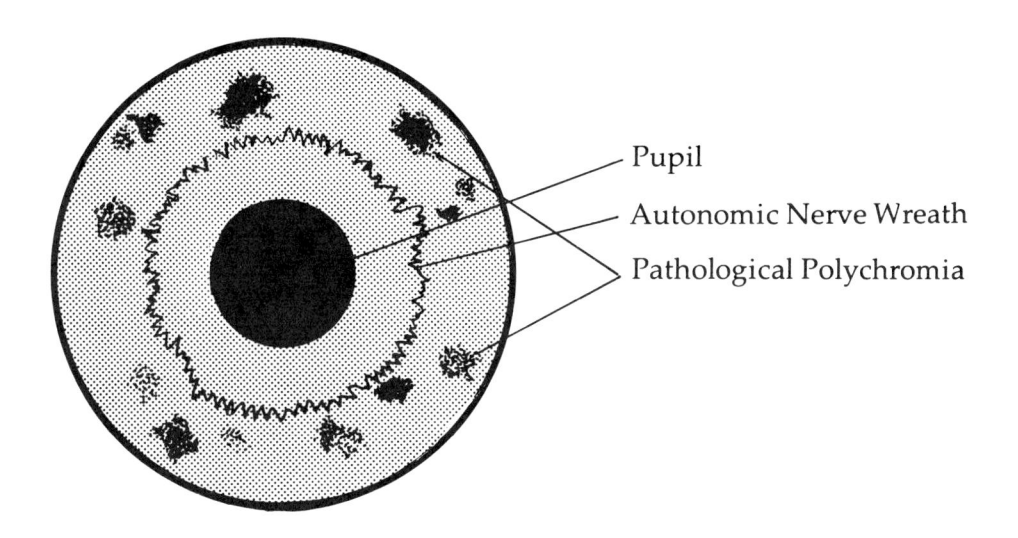

PATHOLOGICAL POLYCHROMIA

- Pupil
- Autonomic Nerve Wreath
- Pathological Polychromia

In addition to the pigmentation changes of inflammation there are certain pigmentations that appear on the iris surface at random. These had been thought in the past to be drug/mineral deposits in the tissue, but microscopic examination during cadaveral research indicates these to be deposits of various enzymes such as LDH, SGOT and others that are associated with organ cell damage. These pigmentations are termed "Pathological Polychromia".

Upon a superficial iris examination they often appear to look as though they are freckles. This area of iris analysis has, at least until recently, probably caused more confusion than any other. This is because people were being told they had a certain drug deposit in a certain area when many of them had never taken drugs or if they had never taken the ones that supposedly were being seen in their eyes.

This confusion has all been cleared-up now because it is known these are not drug/mineral deposits at all. That is the benefit of research (especially cadaveral) in the verification of these signs.

The color of these pigmentations is significant in determining which organs are involved, but the pigmentation position on the iris is of no importance. Four major pigmentations:

    Dark brown: Hepatotrophic
    Reddish brown: Porphyrin destruction—indicating some

type of a hemalytic/blood destructive condition
Orange: Pancreatic
Yellow: Nephrotic/Kidneys

The emphasis should not now be on the spots, but instead, on the organ that caused them.

Treatment Considerations

Most of these spots will stay long after the organ which caused them has been refortified. They can usually be removed by the use of an eyewash made from the Eyebright herb. The way this eyewash can be used is by emptying one capusle of the Eyebright combination into a cup. Pour in 8 oz. of hot distilled water. Let it steep for eight to ten minutes, strain the mixture through a cotton cloth, let it cool, then wash out the eyes.

Treatment for each of the colors will be discussed with each organ they indicate.

The pigmentation color/organs listed are all discussed somewhere in this text with the exception of the pancreas, therfore herbal combinations for the pancreas are as follows: Golden Seal, Cedar Berries, Uva Ursi, Mullein, Blue Berry, Bistort, Buchu, Comfrey, Dandelion, Yarrow, Garlic, Marshmellow, Capsicum, Licorice.

or:

Cedar Berries, Uva Ursi, Licorice, Mullein, Capsicum, Golden Seal

Alfalfa as a single herb is excellent to be used in conjunction with either of these combinations.

SECTORAL HETECHROMIA

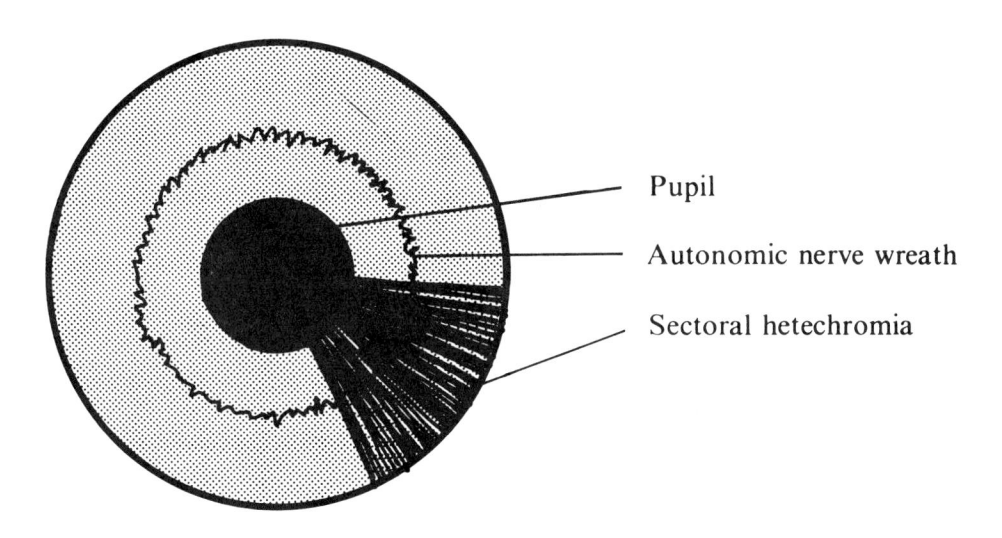

- Pupil
- Autonomic nerve wreath
- Sectoral hetechromia

Sectoral hetechromia is the large area of a different color often seen in the eye. This can be in both eyes but is usually predominant in only one eye. The name is very descriptive—sectoral-section, hete-different, chromia-color, or a section of a different color.

Sectoral hetechromia is significant because it represents an area of the body where either a drug, heavy metal, or inorganic substance has settled. This material is a part of the tissue in that area and shows very specifically in the iris. The area affected shows the discoloration as an actual part of the fibers and in some cases it will be so entrenched in the tissue that the iris fibers themselves will not be discernable in that area.

It has often been said that this is caused by just drugs, but it can be anything chemical that the body has been unable to eliminate and thus has stored in the tissue. It is this sign in the parent that leads to what has been termed the "psoric spot" in the child.

If heavy metal poisoning such as lead or mercury is suspected, the Doctor should examine the gum line of the patient for indicating signs. A hair/mineral analysis is very successful in identifying exactly which metal is involved, if in fact a metal has been deposited.

Treatment Considerations

Recommended treatment for a person showing this sign should be to take them off regular water and place them on distilled water. They should also be placed on a blood purifier such as: Red Clover, Burdock, Yellow Dock, Yarrow, Dandelion, Licorice, Chaparrel, Cascara Sagrada, Barberry, Sarsaparilla.

or:

Gentian, Catnip, Golden Seal, May Apple, Barberry Bark, Myrrh Gum, Yellow Dock, Comfrey, Irish Moss, Fenugreek, Pink Root, Chickweed, Black Walnut, Dandelion, Safflowers, St. Johnsworth, Echinacea, Poke Root, Cyani Flowers.

Horsetail Grass is effective single herb booster for this condition.

LYMPHATIC TOPHI

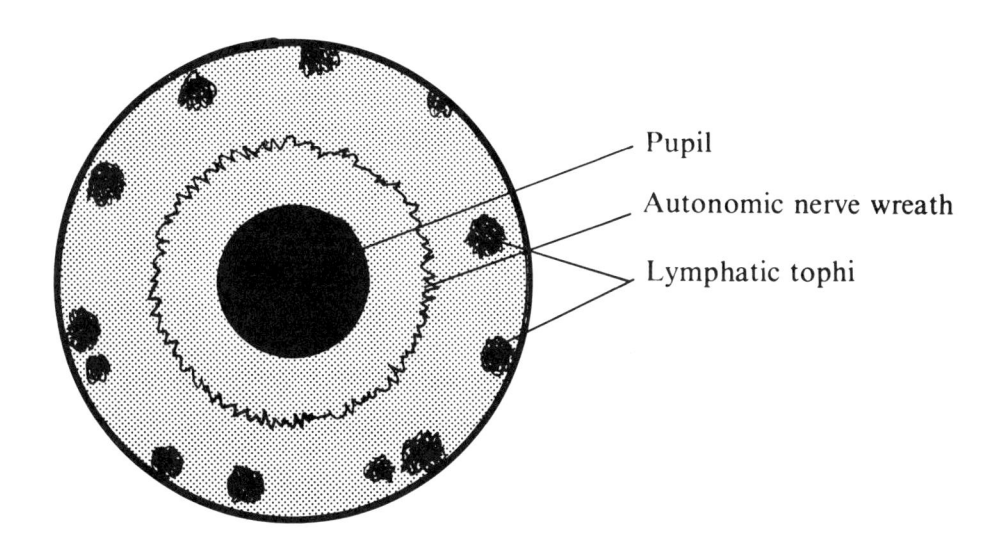

Pupil
Autonomic nerve wreath
Lymphatic tophi

The lymphatic system is one of the systems of the body that man knows very little of. In fact, it was just discovered last year by the Russians that man actually has two hearts. The first one being to pump the blood through the system and the second being a pump for the lymphatic system.

The lymphatics play many important roles in our bodies. Their inability to perform their designed functions will lead to the death of the organism very soon.

The lymphatic system is the protective and defense system of the body as well as the system that helps the absorption of the fat soluble vitamins D, A, K, and E.

This system also helps to purify the blood and returns very important plasma proteins back into the blood that would otherwise be lost in the body.

The lymphatic system has many little elements physically in the lymphatic zone of the iris. These are usually not seen. However, when they are seen, this is an indication that the *complete* lymphatic system of the body, especially of the head, is extremely congested.

This lymphatic involvement shows itself normally as individual patches or balls of cotton which appear just medial of the circulatory zone. It is not uncommon, as these begin to rupture and drain into their area, to see them join each other and become almost a solid circle in the iris.

To the experienced examiner this does not create a problem. It is based mainly on its irregularity of shape and location. The lymphatic tophi will often appear as various colors. This is indicative of the material of which it is congested with.
Prior to the cadaveral research in Germany, it was thought by most American Iridologists that these tophi were not actual structures of the eye, but instead was a reflexed sign which indicated lymphatic congestion in the neurological part of the iris for which it was found.

Treatment Considerations

Herbal remedies should be a combination of: Plantain, Black Walnut, Golden Seal Root, Marshmallow Root, Bugleweed, and Lobelia. If the patient is a known hypoglycemic, substitute Myrrh Gum for Golden Seal. An alternate formula for hypoglycemics is Echinacea, Myrrh gum, Poke Root and Cayenne. The recommended dosage is one capsule three times a day.

Another very good formula is: Red Clover, Burdock, Yellow Dock, Yarrow, Dandelion, Licorice, Chaparrel, Cascara Sagrada, Barberry, Sarsaparilla.

Rosehips as a single herb is very effective in assisting the body fight infection.

If a very severe infection is present, the patient may be given one capsule per hour plus two capsules of Rose Hips per hour until mild diarrea begins. At that point, the Rose Hip dosage is to be reduced by 50%. Children under twelve do very well on one half the adult dosage for both the lymphatic formula and the Rose Hips.

These combinations will begin stepping up body elimination from both the urinary and the intestinal tract.

Another consideration for cleansing the lymphatic system is any type of exercise that will produce sweating. The "Rebounder", a home exercising unit, when properly used is outstanding for this purpose.

ARCUS SENILIS

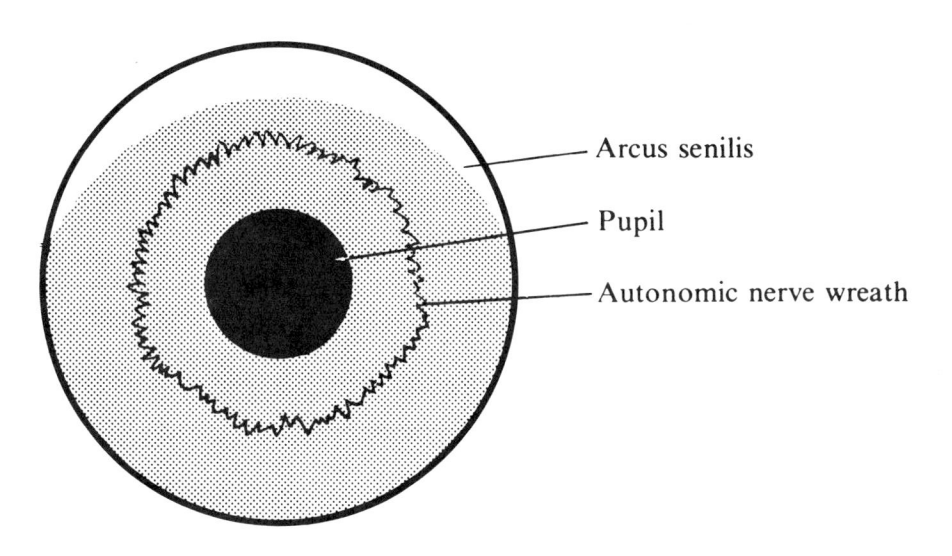

- Arcus senilis
- Pupil
- Autonomic nerve wreath

The arcus senilis sign was at one time only seen in those who are senile or thought to be senile. It is seen as a white hat covering approximately the upper one third of the iris. The white area is on the edge of the iris. This outer area is classed as Zone #6 and is representative of the circulatory zone. Thus it tells what is in the arteries and along the artery walls.

This sign indicates partial blockage in the arteries of the head and neck primarily. These vessels begin to plaque from triglycerides, inorganic sodium, and various other types of material that collect and create a blockage of the arteries. This sign can be seen at any age today and is indicative of a circulatory deficiency to the brain. This reduced blood flow to the brain cells is what is being found to be the cause of senility. It is a very gradual process but detectable through the use of an iris examination.

Note: This sign is being seen with many users because it has a factor that causes fat cells in the blood to clump especially in the arteries of the brain.

Treatment Considerations

Herbal recommendations are Cayenne, Parsley, Ginger, Ginseng, Golden Seal Root, and Garlic. This formula is very good for increasing the blood flow to the brain and also dissolving the build-up of plaque. This will automatically begin to lower high blood pressure. Vitamin E, 800-1000 iu per day, will also enhance the oxygenation of the brain cells.

Another formula is: Blessed Thistle, Peri Winkle, Blue Vervian, Ginger, Capsicum. A B-complex capsule should be taken at least 2-3 times daily. Slant board and rebounding types of exercising are a must with this condition. Exercise should be for no less than 5 minutes twice a day. Exercise again is highly recommended; three to five minutes of gentle exercise on the "Rebounder" or similar exercise unit is very beneficial. This should also be used with exercise; the patient should lie on a slant board five to fifteen minutes two times a day, thus reversing the gravitational pull on the body and allowing an increased blood flow to the brain. This is also very beneficial to all that stand a great deal of the time.

HYPERCHOLESTEROSIS

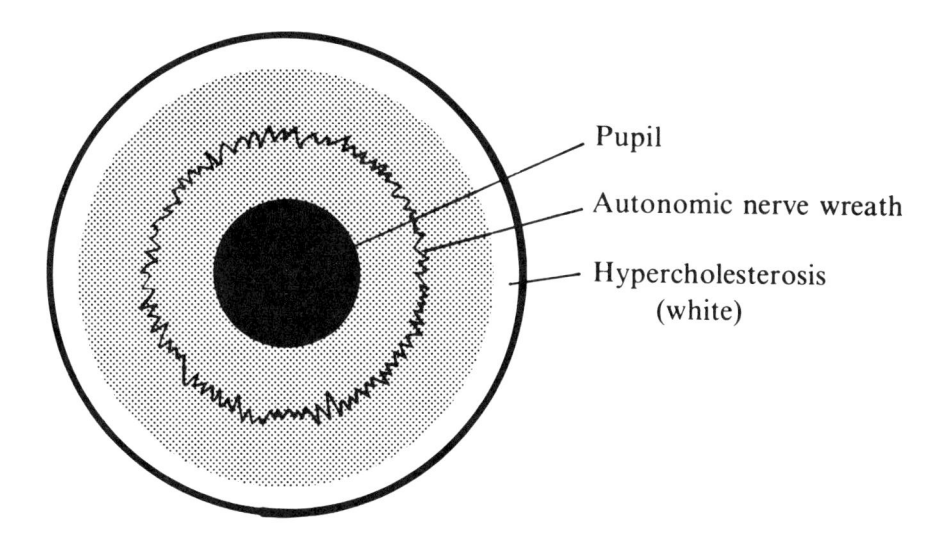

- Pupil
- Autonomic nerve wreath
- Hypercholesterosis (white)

This sign is like the arcus senilis but now extends around the complete eye. The person's vascular system is much more involved now and can creat circulatory blockage anywhere in the body. In the early stages the arteries are said to be atheroscleratic but once this condition has progressed it soon becomes one of arteriosclerosis. The extent of involvement can be estimated by the brilliance of the relfexed light from this area and the thickness of the sign.

The Doctor can further evaluate this condition with lab studies of the lipid triglyceride levels. A major organ here that must be evaluated is the liver, for the liver is the organ that produces these plaquing substances.

Another cause for this plaquing is the storage by the body of inorganic sodium. This can be either from salt or even artificial sweetners. The body, in an effort to rid itself of these items begins to store it in an out-of-the-way place—the arteries. This is what blocks the coronary arteries and causes a caridac infarct. An actual part of the heart muscle dies because it cannot get enough blood to meet its functional demands.

Treatment Considerations
Like the Arcus Senilis, these people require more exercise. Herbal recommendations Cayenne, Parsley, Ginger, Gingseng, Golden

Seal Root, and Garlic. A satisfactory dosage for most adults is two, three times a day. This sign is often seen in the salt user. Salt must be removed from their diet. An organ that usually is highly involved here is the liver. If this is the case, the patient should be put on a blood cleanser. A Red Clover combination works very well for this. This can be taken one, three times a day or up to a point of diarrhea. An excellent combination for the liver is Barberry, Wild Yam, Cramp Bark, Fennel Seed, Ginger, Catnip, and Peppermint. This formula is recommended two, three times a day; along with these herbs a natural source of trace minerals such as that found in Norwegian Kelp should be included with at least three, three times a day.

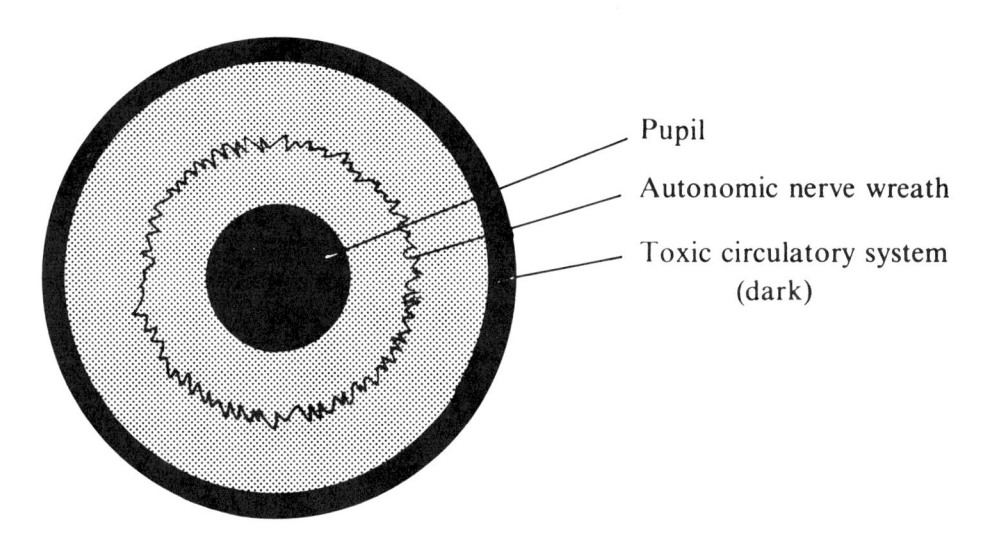

TOXIC CIRCULATORY SYSTEM

Pupil
Autonomic nerve wreath
Toxic circulatory system (dark)

The circulatory system is usually involved in any case of toxicity. It becomes more like a sewer system than a circulatory system. This is because the blood constantly (in a toxic situation) has toxins seeping into it from both the large and small intestines. This material is being carried to all parts of the body.

When considering any condition, it must always be remembered than no matter what organ, tissue, or cell is creating dysfunction, they can never be completely restored by *any means* as long as the blood going to that area is toxic.

When the circulatory system is toxic, the circulatory zone will appear very dark. This is thought to be reflexing from the venous portion of the circulatory system.

Treatment Considerations
The circulatory system will begin cleansing itself very well on any one of several blood cleansers. A combination of Red Clover Blossoms, Chaparral, Licorice Root, Poke Root, Peach Bark, Oregon Grape, Stillingia, Cascara Sagrada, Sarsaparilla, Prickly Ash Bark, Burdock Root, and Buckthorn Bark. This combination can be used either as a tea or taken in capsule form. The capsules are used one, three times a day for most people or one cup of tea three times a day.

Another outstanding blood purifier is: Red Clover, Burdock, Yellow Dock, Yarrow, Dandelion, Licorice, Chaparral, Cascara Sagrada, Barberry, Sarsparilla.

Singel herb boosts: Chaparral or Echinacea. Only one single herb boost should be used. It is normally taken 1-3 times daily.

No blood cleanser should be used at a frequency which will cause diarrhea, although a loose stool may be quite common in most cases.

SCURF RIM

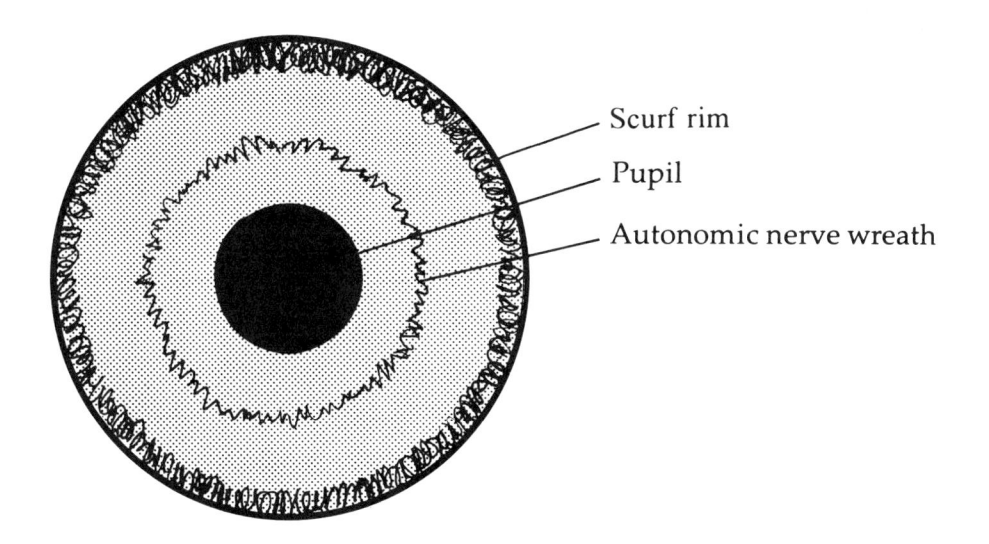

- Scurf rim
- Pupil
- Autonomic nerve wreath

The very outside of the iris is representative of the skin. Whenever the skin becomes weak or involved in being unable to shed its outer coat, epidermis (which is dead skin), the skin becomes very congested. This congestion is reflexed into the iris as looking a bit cloudy, scurfy around the iris, thus the term scurf ring/rim.

The skin (even though not usually thought as such) is the largest organ of the body. The skin becomes very susceptible to what is occurring on the outside of it as well as the inside. On the *outside* it is constantly being abused by soaps and creams that clog the pores and in many cases cause much localized irritation. On the *inside*, the skin is a source of drainage for toxic materials that cannot escape through the normal channels. Thus many skin conditions are caused by various eliminating organs not preforming their job adequately and the skin must try to secrete the overload. This is especially true for the kidneys. If the kidneys are not eliminating its acids adequately, especially uric acid, the person will develop open, running sores on the skin that in many cases even smell like urine.

The skin is involved in temperature control. It opens its pores to allow perspiration out to cool us when we become overheated and closes its pores to maintain our body temperature. The skin is also involved in respiration and its intake is considered in our total air volume.

Treatment Considerations

When considering treating the skin, one must first insure that all of the organs of elimination are functioning adequately, (kidneys, lungs and alimentary tract).

Only a very pure soap should ever be used on the skin. I prefer a soap made of Vitamins E, A, and D. The person should lather up very well with this soap each time it is used. They should be taking at least two showers daily, morning and evening. Prior to their shower the skin should be brushed with a luffa or a dry rough washcloth. There are also some very good skin brushes which can be purchased at most health food stores.

The shower should be started with warm water then increase to hot. Stay in that temperature long enough to produce a good sweat, lather during this period, then rinse and decrease the water temp-erature to cool and finish with cold. This allows the skin to go through its complete cycle of opening and closing.

A person having a skin problem is usually quite deficient in the B-complexes. B-complex tablets should be taken 2-3 times daily.

Another requirement of the skin is for particular minerals and trace minerals that are usually very deficient in the American diet. These being silicon and sulfer. There are several herbal compositions that are very rich in these items. One combination for the skin includes the following herbs: Dandelion Root, Sassafras, Burdock Root, Licorice Root, Echinacea, Yellow Dock Root, Kelp, Cayenne, and Chaparral. This combination of herbs feeds the skin with what that organ requires and at exactly the correct amount. Two, three times a day is usually an adequate amount. Anytime the skin is being fortified, a blood purifier such as Chaparral or Red Clover should be used in conjunction. This can be drunk as a tea either hot or cold several times a day.

Another supporting factor for the skin is the Nedman's clay. this may be made into a paste and applied locally or taken orally by capsules two, three times a day.

Let us not forget what the most supposedly beautiful women in the world used (Cleopa... aloe vera. This may be used both internally and externally in the area of erruption.

There are several alternatives here, but the main thing to remember is that usually the skin problem is a result of something else, not the cause. So find the cause and heal that!

HEALING CRISIS

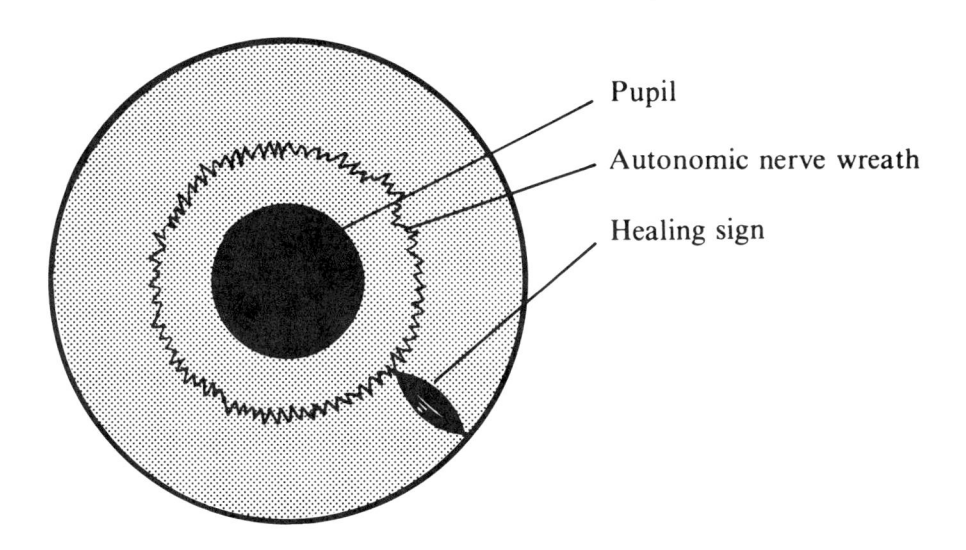

- Pupil
- Autonomic nerve wreath
- Healing sign

When the body is actively fighting a condition there is a temperature increase, pain, and similar symptoms. We know our body is fighting something. If we will just aid our bodies by giving it rest, light nutrition, and increase our elimination, the body will handle the condition and that will be the end of it.

If on the other hand, we interfere and take drugs or other things that force our temperature temporarily down, this inhibits the body from ever getting rid of the original condition completely. Now we have created a chronic state in the area of the original problem. Because of its chronicity, this area will always give us problems until finally strengthened again (by our help) to the point of the increased temperature so that the body can now handle this problem completely, as it should have done in the beginning. The returning of the original condition and symptoms is what is termed a "healing crisis." This is what should be hope for and worked towards with each chronic area of the body.

The reoccurence of these conditions is short-lived and predictble by specific iris signs. This area will be discussed in much more detail in the intermediate text. The fundamental iris material is so voluminous that it suffices for you to be aware of the "healing crisis" up to the degree discussed at this time.

Treatment Considerations

A natural source of vitamin and minerals should be supplied to the body during this time insuring it has all the raw material necessary. An excellent herb formula for this is: Parsley, Watercress, Kelp, Irish Moss, Black Walnut, Sarsaparilla, Iceland Moss. Alfalfa should also be taken as a single herb boost.

In conjunction to the body builders a blood purifier is also necessary to help the body rid itself of the toxins released during the healing crises.

A combination of: Red Clover, Burdock, Yellow Dock, Yarrow, Dandelion, Licorice, Chaparral, Cascara Sagrada, Barberry, Sarsaparrila. The building herbs can be taken as often as possible 3-4 three times a day.

The blood purifier only up to a point just short of diarrhea. Usually 1, three times daily.

CHAPTER IV
Major Organs and Natural Remedies

MAJOR ORGANS

Each of these organs are extremely important and deserve to be studied. These will be studied in depth in the intermediate Iridology text. However, because of their importance, a nutritional consideration will be covered.

Heart: There are several outstanding herbs for the heart. Cardiologists of old had much success and so have I with the use of the Hawthorn Berry Syrup. The Hawthorn Berry is richer in vitamin C than even the Rose Hip. This syrup can be taken as frequently as necessary depending upon the condition. Another very good herb for the heart is Cayenne. Cayenne is food for all smooth muscles plus has the ability, like niacin, to rapidly increase circulation without stressing any of the vascular system. I have seen virtual miracles occur from the use of either of these herbs.

The Cayenne is also very effective as a tincture mixed in warm water. One half teaspoon in 4 oz. of water is quite adequate for most conditions. Cayenne is a pepper and should not be taken in large amounts at one time until the person is quite accustomed to it.

A very good herbal composition is one that contains Hawthorn Berries, Cayenne/Capsicum. I have found with most chronic conditions one, three times a day is adequate. This will naturally vary (as do all of these) for each case. No two people are the same.

Vitamin E and Vitamin B in complex should always be used in conjuction with any formula.

Lungs: The lungs do not normally receive the attention they deserve for the important functions they perform. Herbal compositions with Marshmallow, Mullein, Comfrey, Lobelia, and Chickweed are natural food for the lungs. I have found that patients with decreased respiratory function do very well on this composition at a rate of two, three times a day.

Liver: This is probably the most important organ in our bodies, and probably also the most abused. An herbal composition to rebuild and help detoxify the liver is one containing Barberry, Wild Yam, Cramp Bark, Fennel Seed, Ginger, Catnip, and Peppermint. Another excellent formula for the liver is: Dandelion, Red Beet Powder, Liverworth Leaves, Parsley, Horsetail, Birih Leaves, Lobelia, Chamomile, Blessed Thistle, Yellow Root, Anglica, Gentian, and Golden Rod. The use of these combinations should be increased gradually from one, two times a day to three, three times a day over a period of time.

When working with the liver, the intestinal tract and the circulatory system should also be considered.

Kidneys: Like the liver, this is an organ way over worked. An excellent herbal composition is one that contains Juniper Berries, Parsley, Uva-Ursi, Marshmallow, Lobelia, Ginger, and Golden Seal Root. Chronic kidney weaknesses usually require this to be taken several times per day.

An Herbal potassium should also be used as a booster. A usual adult amount is one, three times a day.

Nervous System: The nervous system is the ultimate control of the complete body (page 4, Grays Anatomy, 23rd Edition, American Version). Thus it is considered to be the most important system.

There are two excellent herbal combinations each accomplishing a different task. The first consists of Black Cohosh, Cayenne, Hops Flowers, Mistletoe, Lobelia, Scullcap, Wood Betony, Lady's Slipper, and Valerian Root. The second is a combination of Horsetail Grass, Oat Straw, Comfrey, and Lobelia. When dealing with this system I have found that a satisfactory amount is one or two, three times a day of the first combination and three, three times a day of the second. B-complex one, three times a day should always be used to support the nervous system.

Most people do not know how to take herbs. Herbs, even though a food, because of their basic state breakdown in the stomach in about one minute. Many of these herbs, although very effective, do not taste very nice. Therefore I recommend that any one taking herbs should take them *between* meals and not directly after a meal. These can be taken with either water, milk, vegetable juice, etc.

I have mentioned the importance of the nervous system in controlling the body, however, it should also be realized that no matter what organ or system we are dealing with, it cannot function properly without a normal nerve supply. The nerve supply to each area must be at its prime. I cannot stress the importance of this enough.

CHAPTER V
Case Studies

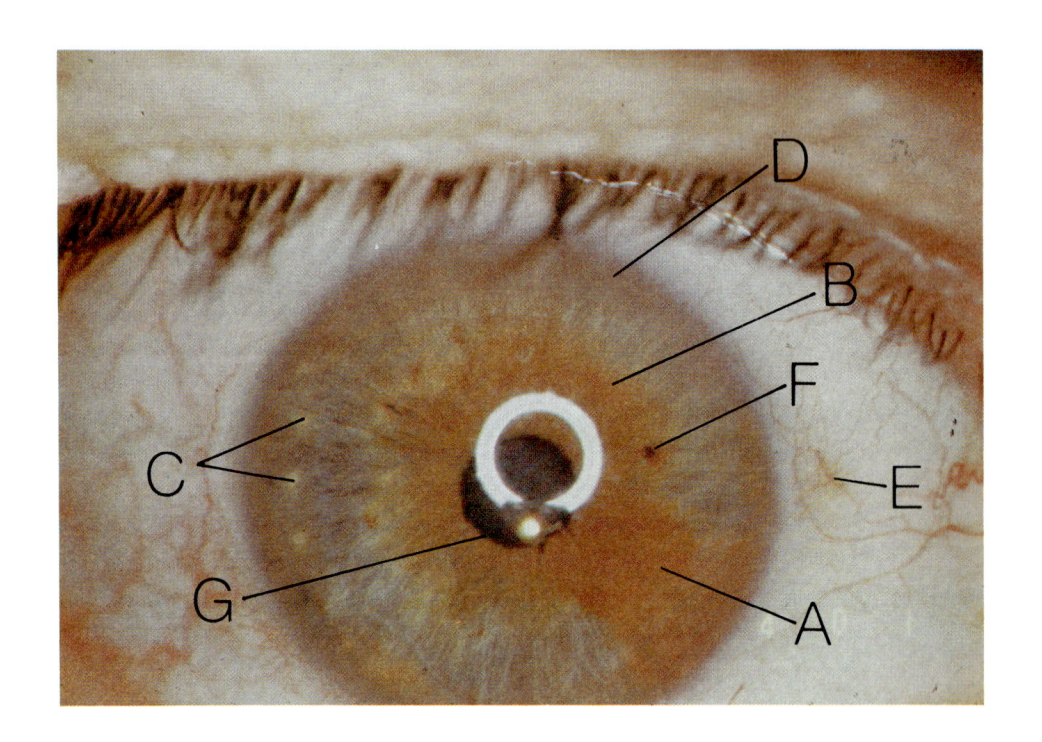

A. Sectoral Hetechromia
B. Toxic Colon
C. Lymphatic Tophi
D. Arcus Senilis
E. Lipid/Fat Deposits
F. Pathological Polychromia
G. Nerve-Root Pressure

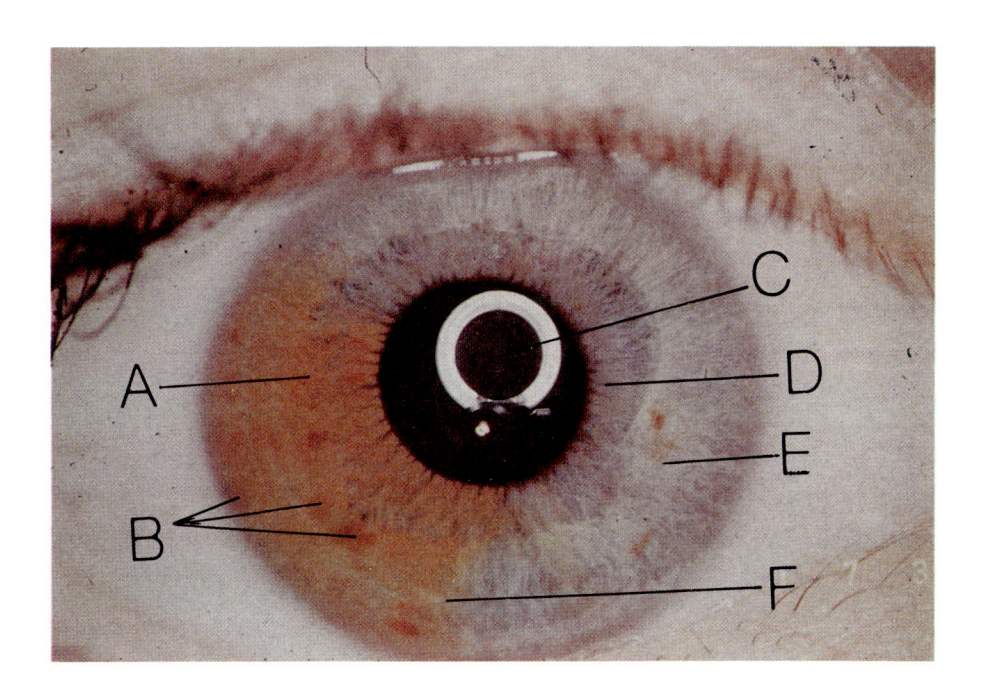

A. Sectoral Hetechromia
B. Pathological Polychromia
C. Adrenal Stress
D. Hyperactive Stomach
E. Increased Tissue Acidity
F. Psychological Stress Rings

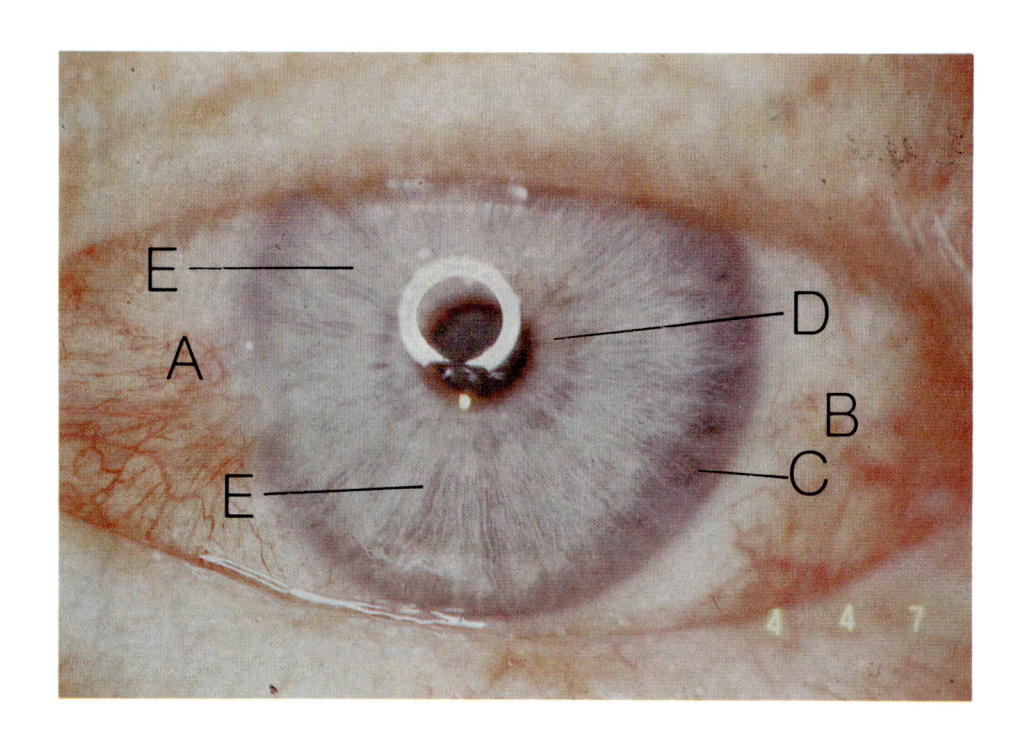

- A. Pterygium
- B. Lipid/Fat Deposits
- C. Ischemia
- D. Hyperactive Stomach
- E. Increased Tissue Acidity

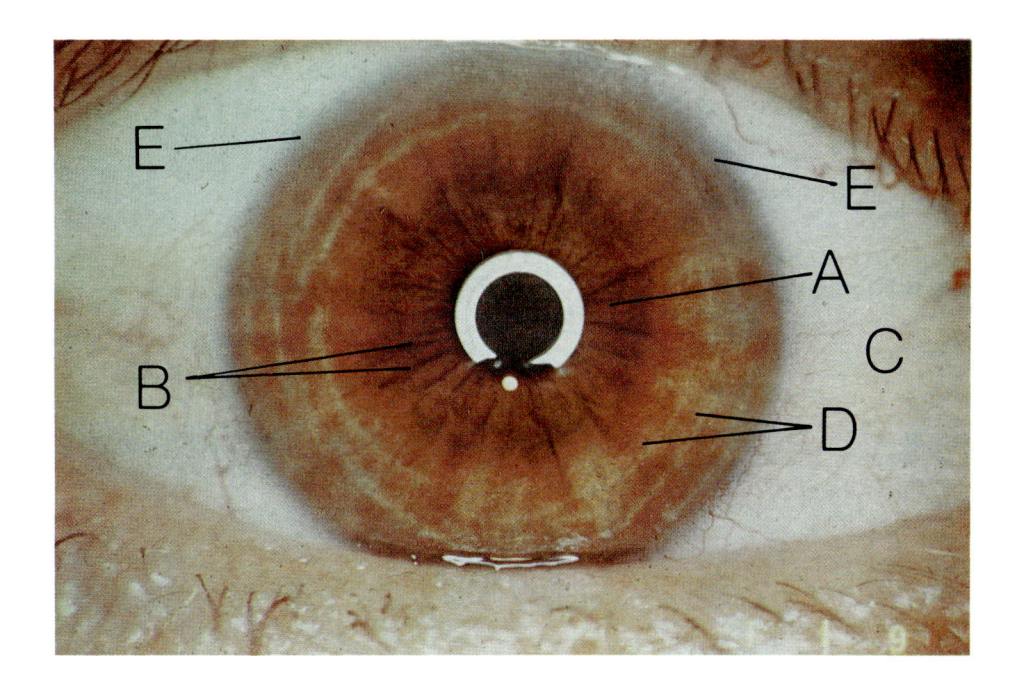

A. Toxic Colon
B. Radii Solaris
C. Lipid/Fat Deposits
D. Psychosomatic Stress Rings
E. Arcus Senilis

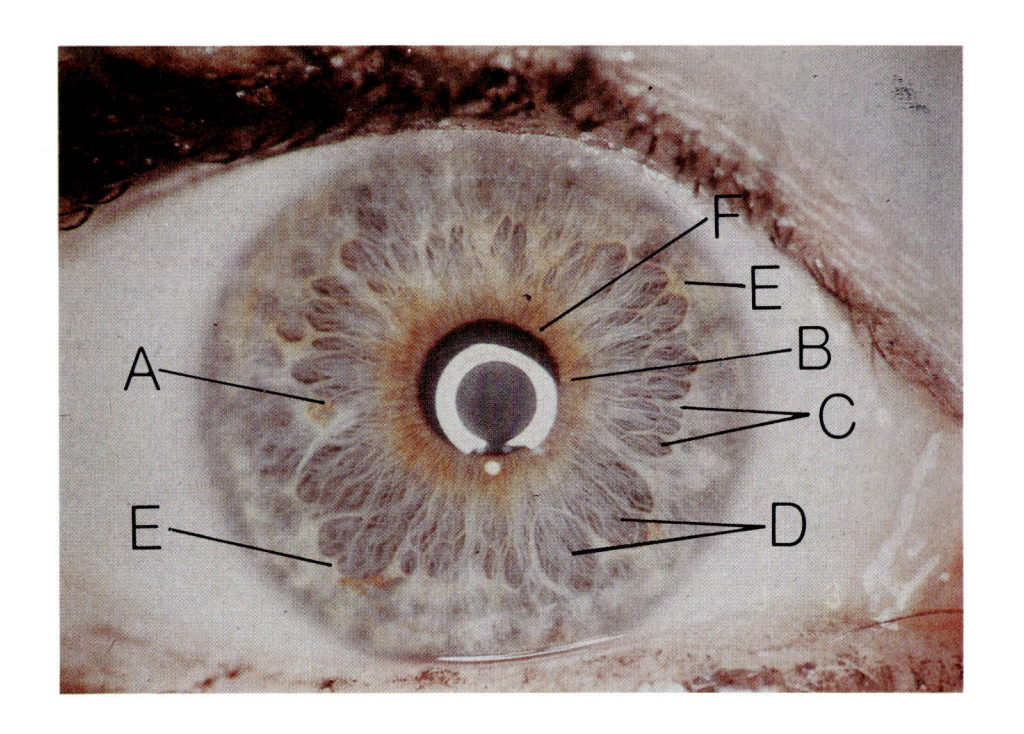

A. Bronchial Inflammation
B. Digestive Chronisity
C. Colon/Large Bowel Dystonia
D. Diverticulosis
E. Lymphatic Tophi
F. Nerve-Root Pressure of the Cranial Bones

CASE STUDY

Headaches and Nervousness

Iris Signs: Toxic Colon and Psychosomatic Stress Rings

This is the slide of a 25 year old woman. Her major complaints were severe headaches which also caused pain in her eyes and extreme anxiety and nervousness. She said that when her eyes begin to hurt, they felt as though they would explode right out of her head. During a headache she became extremely sensitive to light and would have to remain in the dark until the headache was gone, this sometimes took days!

The headaches she described are being caused from her toxic colon radiating toxins to the head and brain. For the colon problem we used a bowel cleanser made of:

Cascara Sagrada, Barberry Bark, Capsicum, Ginger, Lobelia, Red Raspberry, Golden Seal, Fennel, Turkey Rhubarb Root

For the anxiety and nervousness we used two formulas. The first:

Irish Moss, Alfalfa, Horse Tail Grass, Comfrey and Lobelia.

Secondly we used:

Black Cohosh, Capsicum, Hops, Mistle Toe, Lobelia, Scullap, Wood Betony, Lady's Slipper, Valerian

Within two weeks the headaches had stopped and she reported a definite feeling of euphoria. She was kept on all formulas for a total of six months because of the severity of her problem.

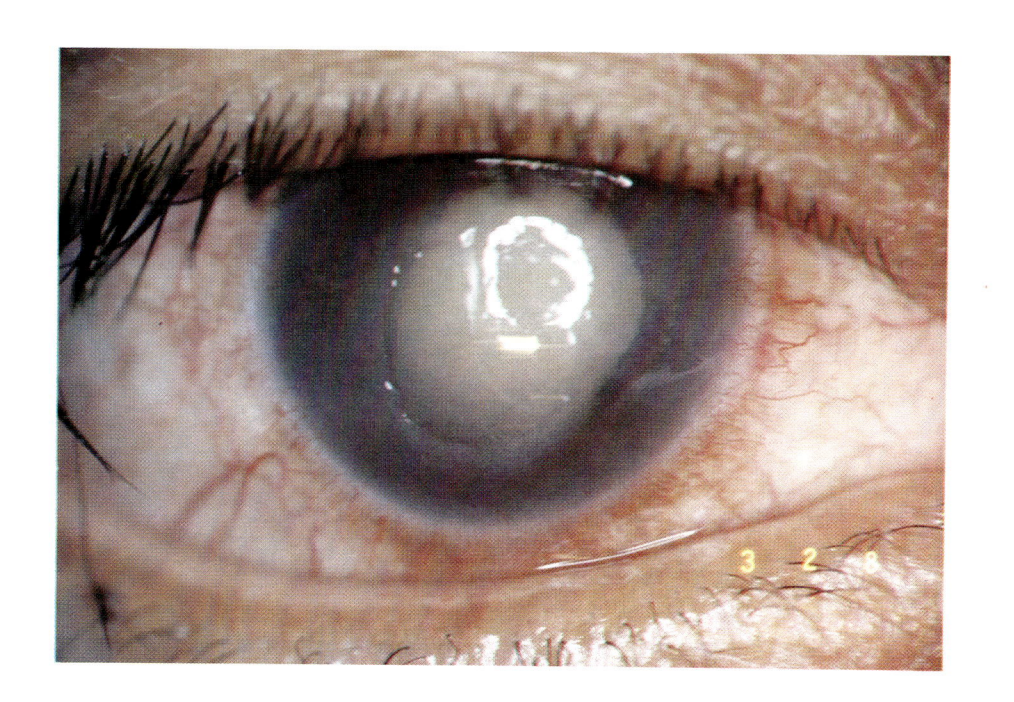

	Chicago, Ill.
CASE STUDY	April 1980

Diabetic Retinopathy

Iris Signs: Color and Shape of Pupil

This is the slide of a man who has been totally blind for 2½ years. His blindness is attributed to a dual cause - diabetes mellitus - creating diabetic retinopathy and glaucoma. His major complaint was not so much the blindness as it was the pain in his eyes. He said the pain was as if he had gravel in his eyes, which created much pain, first only upon opening them, but later all the time.

We began at once with an eyebright herb formula:

(Eyebright, Golden Seal, Bayberry) used both orally and as an eye wash.

Vit. A and D plus the B Complex - both in large dosages.

From the very onset and throughout the treatment, large amounts of pus continually ran from both eyes. He reported a positive change within 24 hours. By the sixth day of using the herbs and receiving spinal care for both the cervical spine and cranial bones, his attitude had become much more cheerful and he said he was even being able to tell by the light changes when his eyes were open and when they were closed.

We allowed him to return home under the care of his local physician who was cooperating very closely with us. We treated this again one month later for four days, at which time he reported, with much glee, that he was beginning to see images and shadows from both eyes.

CASE STUDY

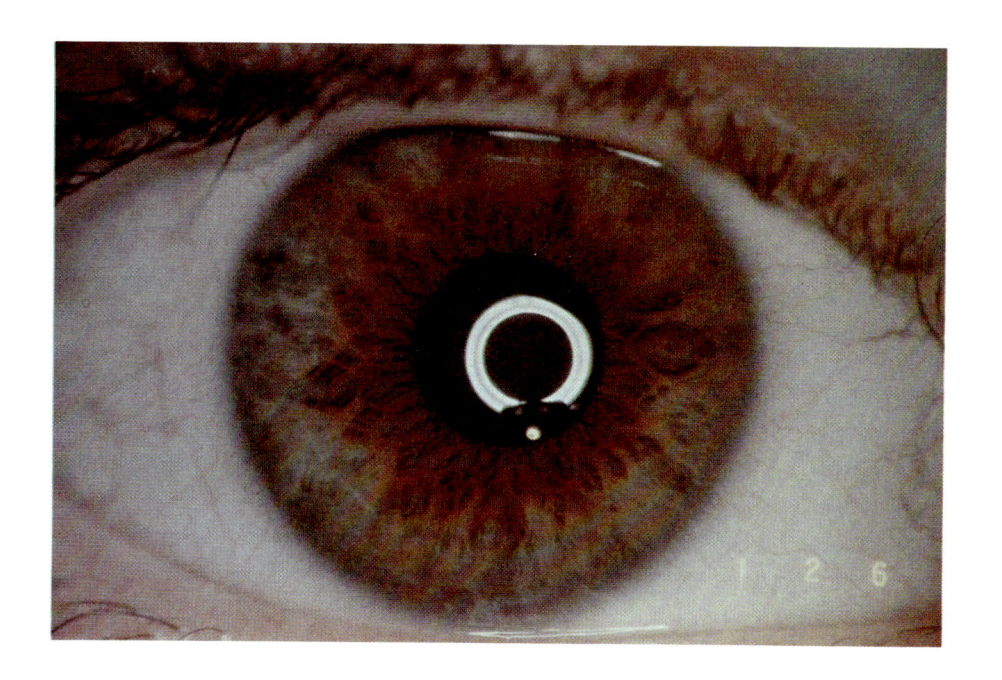

Heart Palpatations
+
Chronic Neuralisia

Iris Signs: Inherited cardiac weakness, severe toxic colon

This is the slide of a 45 year old man who complains of shortness of breath, heart palpatations and flu like pain throughout his entire body.

He had previously been under the care of many heart and arthritis specialist for his problems. He had been placed on medication for his heart, pain killers, diuretics + cortison shots for the chronic pain.

For the heart we used:

Hawthorne Berries and Capsicium + B Complex capsules.

This patient also required spinal manipulation to relieve the excessive spinal pressure at the second thoracic (cardiac) level.

For the toxic/chronic pain, we began a cleansing program of his colon with:

Cascara Sagrada, Bayberry Bark, Capsicuim,
Ginger, Lobelia, Red Rasberry, Golden Seal,
Fennel, Turkey Rhubarb Root.

Within 7 days his heart normalized and within 14 days his arthritic pains were decreased over 50%. After a 90 day program, he no longer had a requirement for medication, is pain free, has normal cardiac function and is on a preventive/maintenance herbal program.

| | Tulsa, OK. |
| | |

CASE STUDY

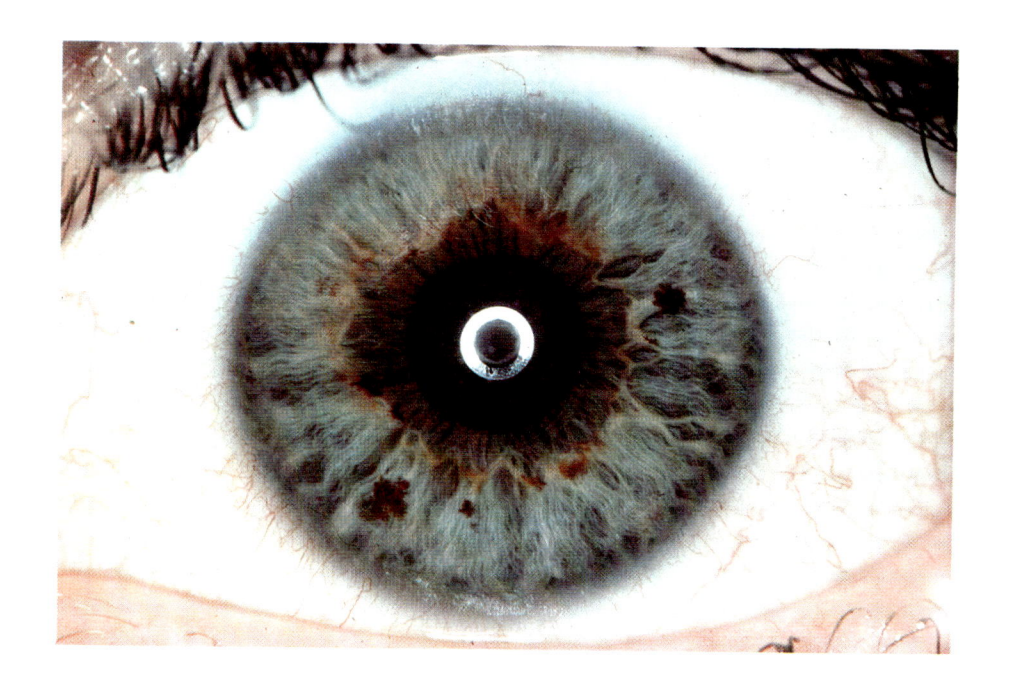

Tulsa, OK.
July, 1979

Iris Signs: Emphasema and Diabetes Mellitus, Liver and Lung Damage, Toxic Colon

This is the slide of a 45 year old man whose major complaint is digestive problems, severe shortness of breath and high blood sugar/diabetes mellitus. He had been under several specialists for his blood sugar problems and was being treated with insulin intravenously twice a day. During this period of time, his blood sugar level was constantly erratic. The blood sugar problem was treated with a formula of:

   Cedar Berries, Uva Ursi, Licorice, Mullein,
   Capsicium, Golden Seal.

The shortness of breath was treated with a long formula of:

   Comfrey, Jullein, Marshmallow, Lobelia
   and Slippery Elm.

The toxic colon was cleaned with a combination of:

Cascara Segrada, Bayberry Bark, Capsicum, Ginger, Lobeilia, Red Rassberry, Golden Seal, Fennel, Turkey Rhubarb Root.

All of these conditions responded very well and in a short period of time, showed to be greatly improved.

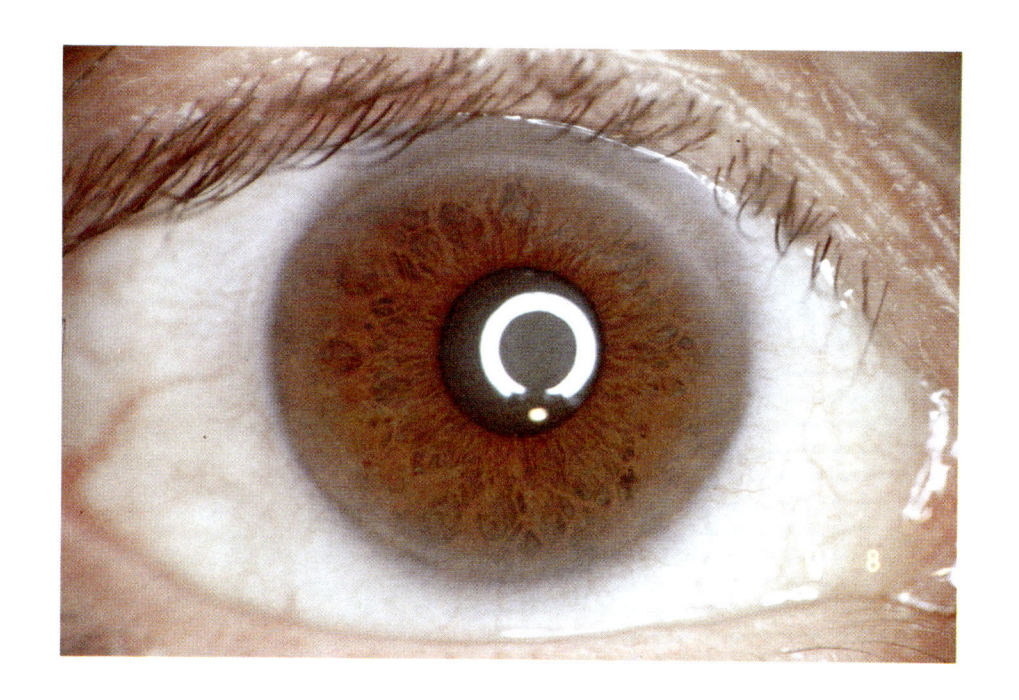

Oklahoma City
CASE STUDY   July 1979

-Senility - Memory-

Iris Sign: Arcus Senilis

This is the slide of a 46 year old woman who complained primarily of confusion, lack of ability to concentrate, and severe forgetfulness. This problem was so severe she even forgot to come into the clinic for her initial appointment on the day she was scheduled.

Because of the partial blockage of the arteries going to the brain, thus reducing the blood supply to the brain, we used a dual approach. First, it was important that we increase the circulation to the brain cells to prevent any further damage. We did this with herbal combination of:

Gotu-Kola, Ginseng and Capsicum.

To begin breaking down the plaquing in the arteries, we used comfrey. Comfrey is gentle and will not overload the kidneys.

This woman continued to improve and after four weeks,

showed a remarkable change. Also, I might add, she never forgot any of her appointments from that time on.

CASE STUDY

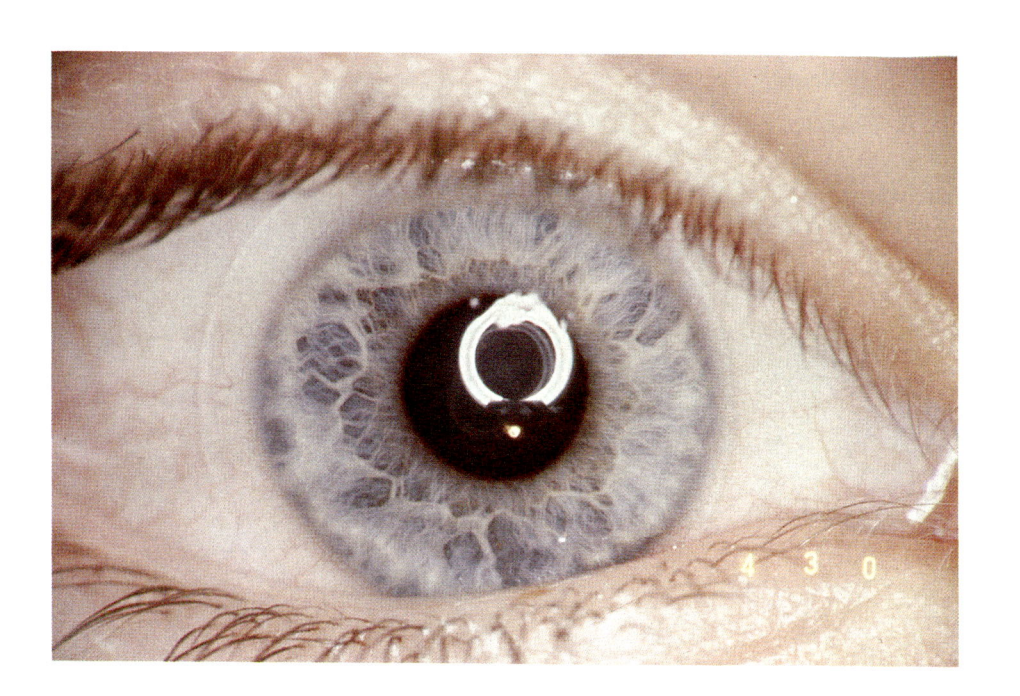

-Hypoglycema and Sinus Allergies-

Iris Signs: Large Pupil, Lung weakness and Tissue Mucus

    This is the slide of a 15 year old girl who complained of being exceptionally low in stamina and felt excessively tired all of the time. Going to school was a great effort and she would sleep almost continuously from after school and late the following morning.
    We used two formulas with this girl. The first contained:

  Licorice, Safflowers, Horseradish

The second formula was:

  Marshmallow, Golden Seal, Chaparral, Burdock,
  Parsley, Cayenne, Lobelia, Brigham Tea

    This girl continued to gain strength, expelled her excess mucus and continued to improve.
    Her parents now complain that they do not see her long enough each day because she is always on the go. She now has a part-time job (after school) a boyfriend and is an active member of three local clubs, not to mention being an honor student at school.

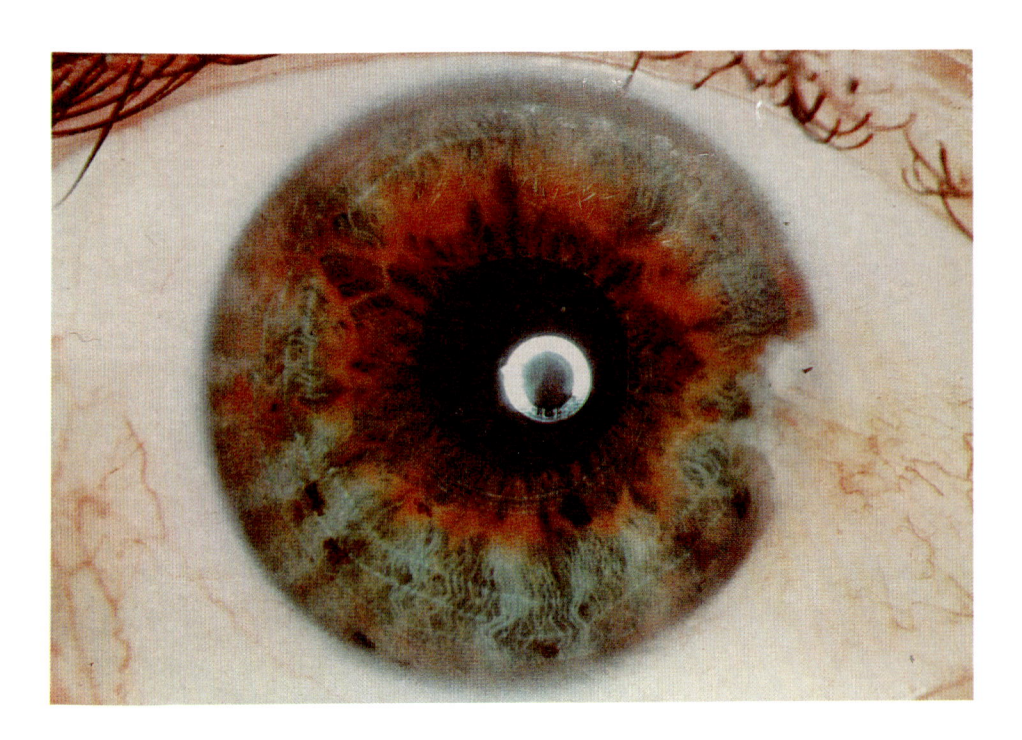

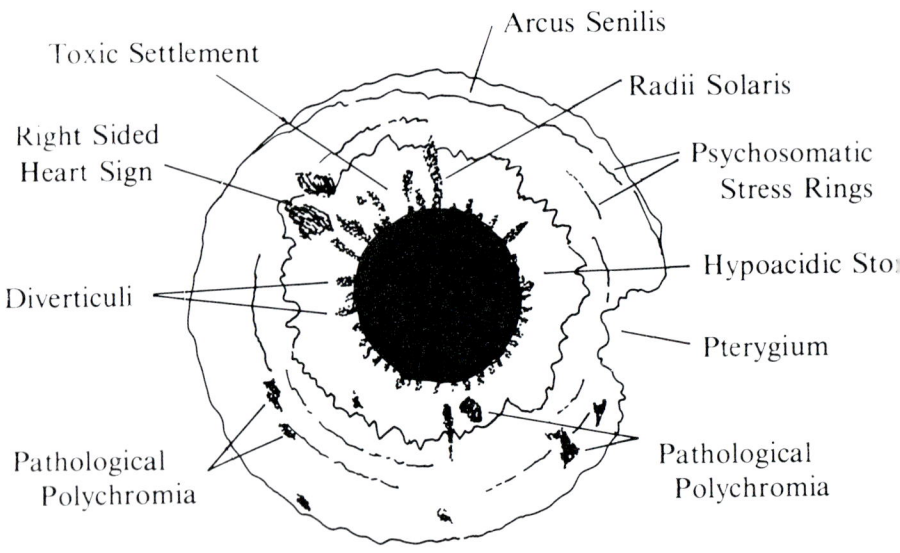

- Arcus Senilis
- Toxic Settlement
- Radii Solaris
- Right Sided Heart Sign
- Psychosomatic Stress Rings
- Diverticuli
- Hypoacidic Sto[mach]
- Pterygium
- Pathological Polychromia
- Pathological Polychromia

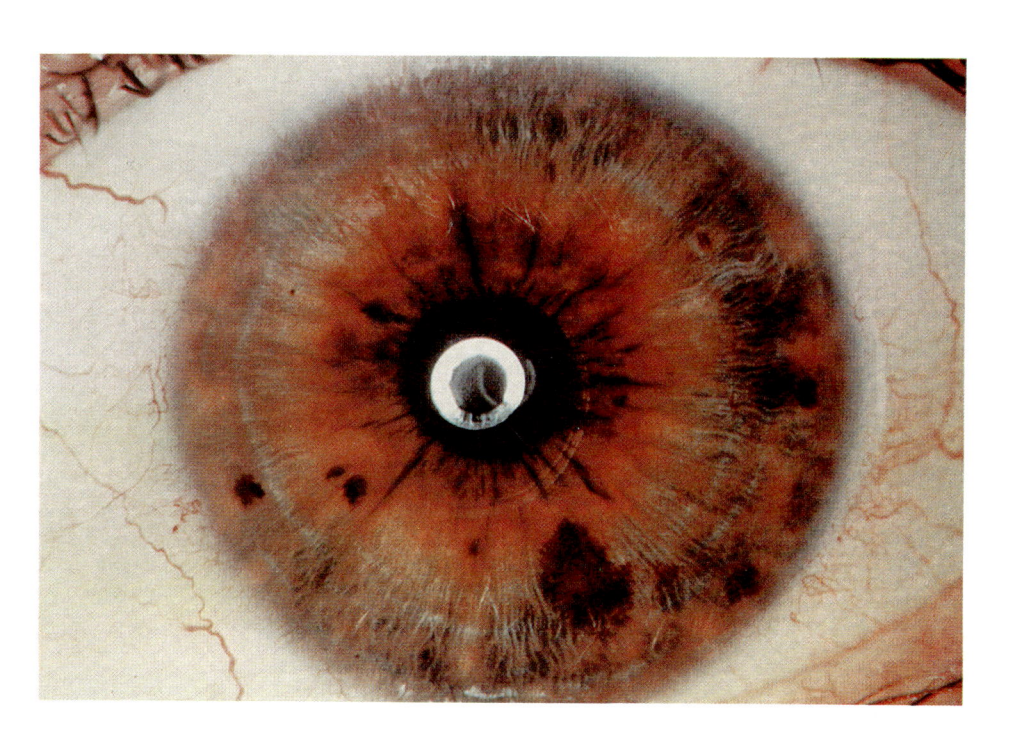

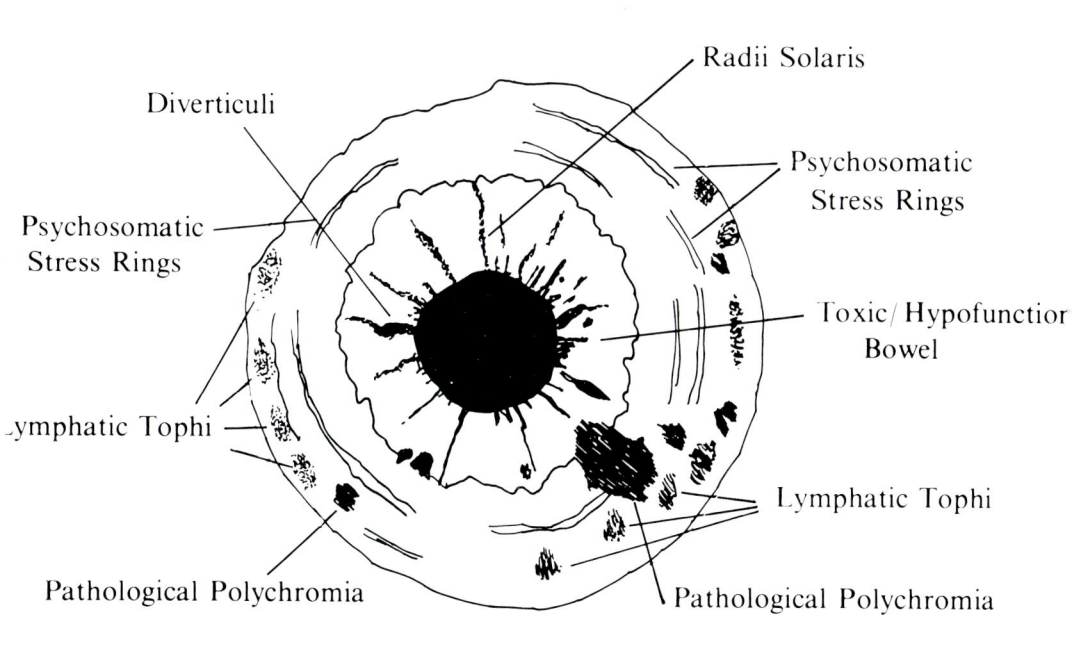

Diverticuli

Radii Solaris

Psychosomatic Stress Rings

Psychosomatic Stress Rings

Lymphatic Tophi

Toxic/Hypofunction Bowel

Lymphatic Tophi

Pathological Polychromia

Pathological Polychromia

REFERENCES

Handbuch der Augendiagnostik, Angerer J., Ph. D., Munich, Germany, 1975

Grundlagen der Irisdiagnostick, Deck, N. D., Ettlingen, Germany, 1965

Gaundbegriffe der Irisdiagnostick, Kriege, Ph. D., 1976

Hergert, M. D., Pigmentation, Munich, Germany

Schimell, M. D., Pigmentation, Munich, Germany

G. Lindemann, Ph. D., Osnabruck, Germany, 1976

Paul H. Steutzer, Ph. D., Texas Chiropractic College, 1978

Rudolph Schnabel, Ph. D., Pigmentation Change

Ophthalmologic Abnormalties, Angerer and Deck, Munich, Germany, 1976

General Ophthalmology, Vaughan, D. and Asbury, T., 1977

Grays Anatomy, 35th British Edition, 1973

Grays Anatomy, 29th American Edition, 1974

Textbook of Medical Physiology, Guyten, Fifth Edition, 1976

Correlative Neuroanatomy and Functional Neurology, 15th Edition, Joseph C. Chusid, 1973

Iridologist International, Volume 1, Issue 3, 1980
The Science and Practice of Iridology, Jensen, 1974

Iridology Discourses, J. Haskel Kritzer, M. D.

Iridology, The Diagnosis From the Eye, Henry E. Lahn, M. D.

INDEX

Underlining denotes major treatment of the subject.
Names of herbs are capitalized.

Acidity, increase in tissues 49
Acute inflammation 23
Adrenal glands 26
Adrenal stress 74
ALFALFA 50, 52, 54, 70, 80
Alkalinity, increase of 51
Allergies, sinus 89
ALOE VERA 35, 68
ANGELICA 72
Antacid 49
Anxiety 79
Aorta 26
Arcus senilis 61, 75, 77, 87
Arteries 87; blockage of 61
Arthritis 50
Autonomic nerve wreath 25, 44
Autonomic nervous system 31

BARBERRY 38, 40, 41, 43, 58, 60, 64, 66, 70, 72, 79
BAYBERRY 81, 84, 86
BISTORT 56
BLACK COHOSH 45, 50, 54, 72, 80
BLACK WALNUT 41, 42, 48, 58, 60, 70
Bladder problems 47
BLESSED THISTLE 62, 72
Blindness 81
Blood sugar 85
BLUE VERVAIN 61
BLUEBERRY 56
Bowel cleanser 37
Bowel dystonia 78
Bowel movements 37
Brain 26; circulation to 61
Brain cells 87
BRIGHAM TEA 89
Bromalin powder 50
Bronchial inflammation 78
Bronchial tubes 26
BUCHU 56
BUCKTHORN 38, 43, 65
BUGLEWEED 60
BURDOCK 50, 58, 60, 65, 66, 68, 70, 89

Calcium deficiency 53
Cancer of the colon 43
CAPSICUM see CAYENNE
Cardiac weakness 83
Caruncle, of the eye 18
CASCARA SAGRADA 37, 38, 40, 41, 43, 58, 60, 65, 66, 70, 79, 84, 86
CATNIP 41, 58, 64, 72
CAYENNE 35, 38, 40, 41, 43, 45, 50, 54, 56, 60-63, 68, 71, 72, 79, 83-87, 89
CEDAR BERRIES 56, 85
CENTAURY 50
CHAMOMILE 52
CHAPARRAL 50, 58, 60, 65, 66, 68, 70, 72, 89
CHICKWEED 41, 48, 58, 71
Chronic conditions 23
Chronic neuralgia 83
Circulatory problems 61, 63
Circulatory system 26; toxic 65
Colon cancer 43
Colon dystonia 78
Colon, prolapsed 47; toxic 37
Color, of iris 7
COMFREY 40-42, 45, 48, 50, 56, 58, 71, 72, 80, 85, 87
Comfrey papain or pepsin 33
Concentration 87
Constitution, somatic 24
COUCHGRASS 38, 43
CRAMP BARK 64, 72
Cranial bones 78, 82
CULVER'S ROOT 40, 42
CYANI FLOWERS 41, 58

DANDELION 41, 52, 56, 58, 60, 66, 68, 70, 72
Degenerative conditions 24
Destructive conditions 24
Diabetes milletus 28, 85
Diabetic retinopathy 81
Digestion dysfunction 33
Digestive chronicity 78
Diverticulitis 37, 43, 78

Douche 48
Drug deposits 55

ECHINACEA 41, 58, 60, 66, 68
Emphysema 85
Eye muscles, and autonomic nerve supply 22
Eyeball, diagram of 19
Eyes, and the iris 21
EYEBRIGHT 56; formula 81

FENNEL 38, 41, 43, 64, 72, 79, 84, 86
FENUGREEK 41, 58
Flatulence 33
Forgetfulness 87

Gall bladder 26
GARLIC 56, 61, 64
Gas 33
Gastric/stomach dysfunction 33
Gastric mucosa 26
Gastro-Intestinal tract 44
GENTIAN 41, 58, 72
GINGER 38, 40, 41, 43, 52, 54, 61-64, 72, 79, 84, 86
GINSENG 61, 62, 87
Glands 28
Glaucoma 81
GOLDEN ROD 72
GOLDEN SEAL 35, 38, 41, 48, 52, 56, 58, 60, 61, 63, 72, 79, 81, 84-86, 89
GOTU KOLA 87

HAWTHORN 71, 83
Headaches 79
Healing crisis 69
Heart 26, 71; palpitaions 83, weaknesses 28, 63
Heartburn 35
Herbal medicines 15
Herbal formulas 37, 40
Hetechromia, sectoral 57
HOPS 45, 54, 72, 80
HORSERADISH 89
HORSETAIL GRASS 45, 54, 58, 72, 80
Hyper-acidity 49
Hyperactive stomach 74, 76
Hyperalkalinity 51
Hypercholesterosis 63
Hypoglycemia 28, 60, 89
Hysterectomy 47

ICELAND MOSS 50, 70
Infections 60

Inflammation, acute 23
Intestines 26, 44
Iridology, description of 11; terminology 9
Iris, interpretation of signs 21
Iris color 7
Iris layers 20
IRISH MOSS 41, 50, 58, 80
Ischemia 76

JUNIPER BERRIES 52, 72

KELP, 50, 52, 64, 68, 70
Kidneys 26, 28, 67, 72, 87

LADY'S SLIPPER 45, 54, 72, 80
LETTUCE 50
LICORICE 38, 56, 60, 65, 66, 68, 70, 85, 89
Ligaments, torn 48
Lipid/fat deposits 75, 76, 77
Liver 26, 29, 63, 71; damage to 85
LIVERWORT 72
LOBELIA 38, 40, 41, 43, 45, 50, 52, 54, 60, 71, 72, 80, 84, 86, 89
Lung damage 85; weaknesses 28, 89
Lungs 23, 71
Lymphatic tophi 59, 75, 78

Malnutrition 33
MARSHMALLOW 48, 52, 56, 60, 71, 72, 85, 89
MAY APPLE 41-42, 58
Memory 87
Metal deposits 57
MISTLETOE 45, 54, 72, 80
Mucus 89
MUULEIN 40, 42, 48, 56, 71, 85
Muscles 48
MYRRH GUM 35, 41, 58, 60

Nausea 33
Nerve-root pressure 75, 78
nervous system 31, 72
Nervousness 26, 79
Neuralgia, chronic 83

OAT STRAW 45, 72
Opthalmic-somatic analysis 12
OREGON GRAPE
Organ signs, description 27, 28
Oxygen 23

Palpabrae, of the eye 18
Pancreas 26
Papaya/mint 34
Parasites, control of 40
Parasite activity 39, 42
Parasympathetic nervous system 31
Parathyroid 26
PARSLEY 50, 52, 61, 63, 70, 72, 89
Pathological polychromia 55, 74, 75
Pattern changes, in iridology 24
PLACH BARK 65
Peczely, Ignatz, discovery of iridology 11
Peristaltic activity 37
Pelvic organs 48
PEPPERMINT 64, 72
PERIWINKLE 61
Pigmentation, of the iris 55
PINK ROOT 41, 58
Pituitary gland 26
PLANTAIN 60
POKE BERRIES 50
POKE ROOT 40-42, 58, 60, 65
Polychromia, pathological 55
Potassium 51
PRICKLY ASH BARK 65
Prolapsed colon 47
Prostate 47
Psychological stress rings 53, 74, 77, 79
Pterygium 76
PUMPKIN SEED 40, 42
Pupillary changes 18, 31

Radial furrows 41
Radii solaris 39, 77
Reboundology 60, 62
RED BEET POWDER 72
RED CLOVER 38, 43, 58, 60, 65, 66, 68, 70; combination 64
RED RASPBERRY 38, 40, 41, 43, 79, 84, 86
Reproductive organs 26
Rheumatoid arthritis 50
Romaine lettuce 50
ROSEHIPS 48, 54, 60

SAFFLOWER 41, 58, 89
Salt, use of 64
SARSAPARILLA 58, 60, 65, 66, 70
SASSAFRAS 68

Sclera, of the eye 18
SCULLCAP 45, 54, 72, 80
Scurf rim 67
Sectoral hetechromia 57, 74, 75
Senility 61, 87
Septicemia 39
Sinus allergies 89
Skin problems 67
SLIPPERY ELM 40, 42, 48, 85
Sodium 51; natural 49
Solar plexis 26
Somatic constitution 24
Spinal adjustments 48
Spine 26
Spleen 26
SQUAW VINE 48
ST. JOHNSWORT 41, 54, 58
STILLINGIA 65
Stomach 44; hyper-active 35; hypo-active 33
Stomach ring 33
Strength 89
Stress rings 53
Subacute conditions 23
Sweat glands 26
Sympathetic nervous system 31

Tendons, torn 48
Thyroid 26
Tissue acidity 49, 74, 76
Tophi, lymphatic 60
Toxic circulatory system 65
Toxic colon 37, 75, 77, 79, 83, 85
Trace minerals 64
Transverse colon 47
TURKEY RHUBARB 38, 40, 41, 43, 79, 84, 86
Turnip tops 50

Ulcers 35
Uterine/prostate 26
Uterus 47
UVA URSI 52, 56, 72, 85

Vaginal problems 47
VALERIAN 45, 54, 72, 80
Vascular system 63
VIOLET LEAVES 40, 42

Watercress 50, 70
Weaknesses, structural 28
WHITE OAK BARK 48
WILD LETTUCE 54
WILD YAM 64, 72
WITCH HAZEL BARK 40, 42

WOOD BETONY   45, 54, 72, 80

YARROW   50, 56, 58, 60, 66, 70
YELLOW DOCK   41, 48, 58, 60, 66, 68, 70
YELLOW ROOT   72
YUCCA   50

Zones, of the iris   26